WALKING THE
SOUTH WEST COAST PATH
•A COMPANION GUIDE•

COMPILED BY SIMON BUTLER
FROM AN ORIGINAL TEXT BY
PHILIP CARTER

First published in Great Britain in 2015
reprinted 2015

Text © 2015 Simon Butler and Philip Carter
Aerial photography Jason Hawkes 2009, 2015
Historic photos from the Halsgrove Archive

A CIP catalogue record for this book is available
from the British Library.

ISBN 978 0 85710 097 9

PiXZ Books
Halsgrove House, Ryelands Business Park,
Bagley Road, Wellington, Somerset TA21 9PZ
Tel: 01823 653777
Fax: 01823 216796
email: sales@halsgrove.com

An imprint of Halstar Ltd, part of the
Halsgrove group of companies
Information on all Halsgrove titles is
available at: www.halsgrove.com

Printed and bound in China by
Everbest Printing Co Ltd

DEDICATION

In fond memory of Philip Carter

Front cover: *The South West Coast
Path at Wringapeak near Woody Bay
in North Devon; beyond lies Foreland
Point, with Lee Abbey and The Valley
of Rocks in the middle distance.*
© Shirley and Mike Hesman

CONTENTS

South West Coast Path

NATIONAL TRAIL

Legend

- South West Coast Path National Trail
- Heritage Coast
- World Heritage Site
- Area of Outstanding Natural Beauty
- National Park
- UNESCO World Biosphere Reserve
- Public Transport Hub
- County Boundary

N

SOMERSET

DORSET

DEVON

CORNWALL

Exmoor National Park

Dartmoor National Park

Taunton

Minehead
Hurlstone Point
Foreland Point
Great Hangman
Ilfracombe
Morte Point
Braunton Burrows
Northam Burrows
Barnstaple
Bideford
Hartland Point
Higher Sharpnose Point
Bude Bay
Tintagel Head
Trevose Head
Bedruthan Steps
Newquay
St Agnes Head
Godrevy Island
St Ives
Penzance
Cape Cornwall
Land's End
St Michael's Mount
Mount's Bay
Lizard Point
Helston
Truro
Falmouth
Pendennis Point
Nare Head
The Dodman
Gribbin Head
St Austell
Wadebridge
Rame Head
Plymouth
Burgh Island
Bolt Tail
Bolt Head
Kingsbridge
Prawle Point
Start Point
Totnes
Torquay
Newton Abbot
Berry Head
Teignmouth
Dawlish
Exmouth
Exeter
Sidmouth
Axminster
Lyme Regis
Beer Head
Lyme Bay
Golden Cap
Bridport
The Fleet
Dorchester
Weymouth
Portland Bill
Poole
South Haven Point
Old Harry
Durlston Head
Swanage
St Adhelm's Head
Lulworth Cove

Map courtesy of South West Coast Path Association

4

INTRODUCTION

This companion guide to the South West Coast Path is intended to provide added pleasure and knowledge for those have walked it in whole or in part, or those who are planning to walk it. It is based on the book *Exploring the South West Coast Path* by the late Philip Carter who, in 1973, was a founding member of the South West Way Association whose annual publication remains essential reading.

In this companion guide, alongside spectacular aerial photographs, we have added historic photos and information that paint a picture of the places found along the coastal route as they were in bygone days. This background information will enhance the readers's experience of their walk, long or short, helping them visualise the small villages, seaside towns and ports through which they pass, as they looked in earlier times. Philip's death in 2011 brought to an end a life devoted to the creation of the SWCP as we know it today. His enthusiasm and knowledge shine through in the Foreword he wrote for his original book:

The lighthouse on the Breakwater at the entrance to Plymouth Sound. The Breakwater took 30 years to build; it could be said to be the equivalent in engineering terms of the Channel Tunnel of its day. It was built to protect Plymouth Sound from the prevailing south-westerly weather. Until it was built the fleet had to use Torbay as an alternative supply base when the weather was unfavourable at Plymouth.

Many folk have discovered the South West Coast Path by walking a section of it, some indeed with intent, but quite a few others have simply stumbled across it whilst on holiday. Maybe its long-drawn-out gestation and the lack of understanding of those who were supposed to be developing it has mitigated against it being as well known as it should be. However, despite all the false starts the path is now there. One can walk the whole 630 miles from Mine-head to Poole Harbour. Improvements are still needed but the longest footpath in the British Isles awaits those few who wish to walk the whole and those many who would walk a section.

Because the path is so long no attempt will be made in this work to describe it in detail as a step-by-step guide. However where there are worthwhile circular or particular stretches of superb walking these will be mentioned. As an aside, I used to be Secretary to the Coast Path Association and it was said that I had to know every mile of the path. My wife a far more practical person knew every tea shop!

At the end of each chapter there are 'Suggestions for Short Walks'. These have been chosen to give a taste of what the Coast Path has to offer. They obviously have a geographical spread but they have also been chosen to give a variety of scenery and interest. They are intended generally as an easy introduction, so that the tougher, wilder, but often most spectacular sections are missing.

For those who do not know, there follows the answer to some basic questions:

What is a Long Distance Footpath or National Trail? It is a continuous right of way, or right of passage, for those who wish to walk, to be able to make an extended journey on foot, lasting if they wish for at least several days. As far as possible the route should eschew roads and be out in scenic and interesting countryside.

How did such routes come about? They have been around in a number of other countries for some while longer, for instance Sweden had one before World War I, but in the UK they were set up by The Access to the Countryside Act of 1949. (This was the same act that had the enabling legislation to set up our National Parks.) Some of the paths were based on a geographical themes e.g. The Pennine Way. The Offa's Dyke Path has archaeological roots. Our own South West Coast Path has its origins in the fact that the coast used to be regularly patrolled on foot by revenue men to prevent smuggling. There will be further references to the original use in the text below.

St Nicholas Chapel at Ilfracombe on Lantern Hill. Ilfracombe was slow to develop into a resort compared to places in South Devon. The Rev. John Sweet was surprised to find only one bathing machine when he visited here around 1800.

Where does our path go? It encompasses most of the peninsula of South West England. It starts at Minehead in Somerset and stays in that county for only a few miles. It traverses all North Devon. It circumnavigates Cornwall, turning left at Land's End. It continues through all of South Devon and then takes

in nearly all of Dorset to finish at South Haven Point at the seaward end of the south side of Poole Harbour.

How long is it? It is no less than 630 miles, or if you prefer metric 1015 kilometres. It is quite the longest Long Distance Foot-path in the United Kingdom. Statistics tend to pall but one other that is worth repeating is that the total climb for anyone completing the whole path is no less than 115 000 feet, or 35 030 metres. This is very close to ascending Mount Everest from sea level four times! However this fact should not deter, whilst there are very tough sections there are also very easy ones. You can 'pick' and have no need to 'mix'!

How can I find out more about the South West Coast Path? The best source is the South West Coast Path Association – the walker representative organization and a registered charity. The Association writes and publishes annually an up-dated guide to the whole 630 miles of the South West Coast Path. The actual route is described with average timings for each section that is also graded to indicate the physical effort required. The book provides information on bus details; ferry crossings; tide tables and also contains hundreds of walker-friendly B&Bs and campsites on the trail. The Association also produces 53 individual path descriptions each roughly of a day's walk, which describe the South West Coast Path in greater details than the annual guide does. They are also happy to answer specific enquiries. Please feel free to contact the South West Coast Path Association (Registered Charity No.266754) at Bowker House, Lee Mill Bridge, Ivybridge, Devon, PL21 9EF, telephone: 01752 896237, fax: 01752 893654, email info@swcp.org.uk, website www.swcp.org.uk.

Early tourists to Ilfracombe discover the delights of the Lady's Bathing Cove, 1823.

The photograph above shows the view at Minehead looking towards North Hill in 1874. In the foreground are the wooden groynes erected to help protect the harbour which can be seen in the distance. In
those days ships carried limestone from Wales which was processed in limekilns close to the shore for use
as a fertiliser on the fields. Today Minehead has grown considerably from a sleepy village as the aerial
photograph, also looking towards North Hill, shows. It is from here the South West Coast Path starts its
long journey of 630 miles around the South West peninsula, ending at South Haven Point on the shores
of Poole Harbour in Dorset. This picture shows part of the large holiday complex in the foreground.
Behind is the seafront where the path actually starts, beyond again in the shelter of the hill is the attractive old part of the town.

CHAPTER 1
MINEHEAD TO BARNSTAPLE

This first chapter covers several miles of the Exmoor National Park as far as Combe Martin. From there it proceeds along the North Devon Coast passing Ilfracombe to make a major change of direction at Morte Point where it turns south. Passing Woolacombe and Croyde Bay there is then another change of direction to travel along the north side of the Taw estuary towards Barnstaple. At the Great Hangman close to Combe Martin the path reaches its highest point at 1045 feet (328 meters).

The beginning of the path at Minehead is defined by a sculptured path marker consisting of a pair of hands holding a map. Interestingly this was designed by an art student who won a competition to come up with an appropriate design. It was expected that serious walkers setting out to walk the whole path would take a photograph here and again at the end. However, it is quite obvious from observation that many others, not contemplating 630 miles, also use it as a photo opportunity!

South West Coast Path marker at Minehead

Minehead, despite associations with modern holiday facilities, has ancient roots, as the name derives from

Sailing boats in the old harbour at Minehead c.1900. By this date trade had dwindled to a few vessels but in Queen Elizabeth I's time Minehead was a considerable port with Continental trade in coal, iron, wood and wine. In later centuries it became a notorious centre for smuggling.

Another more distant view of Minehead Harbour. The highlands of Exmoor top right. In 1656 Minehead, together with Ilfracombe, Barnstaple and Bideford petitioned the Admiralty for better protection from pirates.

mynedd the Celtic name for a hill. In the past Minehead was a thriving port. There are records from 1632 of Welsh cattle and sheep being imported from such places as Aberthaw. There was also trade with Ireland. In 1656 Minehead, along with Ilfracombe, Barnstaple and Bideford, were petitioning the Admiralty for better protection from pirates. The reason for this was the trade was sizeable, averaging 6500 cattle and 30 000 sheep a year. Wool was also imported, as a nostalgic piece in the *Gentleman's Magazine* recalled the trade in mid-eighteenth century. 'I very well remember to have seen large droves of horses, laden with wool-packs, almost daily passing our road, going from Minehead to Tiverton and other trading places... there were 1500 to 2000 packs of wool yearly brought over from Ireland to Minehead.'

Daniel Defoe was fulsome in his praise 'Minehead, the best port, and safest harbour, in all these counties, at least, on this side: No ship is so big, but it may come in, and no weather so bad, but the ships are safe when they are in.'

Before leaving Minehead some walkers might like to consider, but then probably rapidly forget, what is called 'Challenge Walking'. The Long Distance Walkers Association (LDWA) holds an annual one hundred-mile event, and in 2004 it started at Minehead. The route that year went along

the coast to Lynton then turned in across Exmoor to finish again at Minehead. The object of the exercise is to complete a hundred mile cross-country route in under 48 hours. The idea is to walk day and night, without sleeping and anyone stopping more than two hours is disqualified. Food is provided along the way at checkpoints but participants have paid for this in advance. Mathematically it may not sound much after all it only means averaging just over two miles an hour. However, if you think it sounds easy, try it one year!

The length of the path through the Exmoor National Park is frankly disappointing, it could be so much better, in that a great deal of it is unnecessarily kept away from the coast. There have been improvements and at last, the path actually starts along the coast but there is still much to be done.

Glenthorne, towards bottom left of the picture, is the first house in Devon on leaving Somerset. It is comparatively modern having been designed and built by the Rev. W. S. Halliday about 1830. Below: A group of young ladies on the lawn above Glenthorne in Edwardian times.

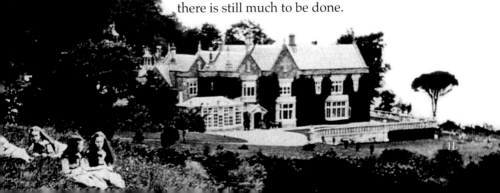

11

Porlock Weir was also once a small port and coal boats unloaded here at least until 1948. Looking back across Porlock Bay towards Hurlestone Point one can see the beach used to represent one near Southampton for the film *The Land Girls*. Such is the filmmaker's art rather than any lack of geographical knowledge! The sea has recently breached the pebble banks of Porlock Bay and it has been decided to let nature take its course and allow the low-lying land behind the banks to become inundated, rather than try to repair the breach.

The descent from Countisbury Hill should not be hurried, as the views ahead to Lynmouth and Lynton are too good. Lynmouth sadly nowadays is more often remembered for the disaster of August 1952 when torrential rains caused the local rivers to overflow, sweeping down their narrow valleys

Above: While much changed from the scene of arround 1900, the village of Porlock lies just inland from the route of the Coast Path and offers hospitality to those walkers looking for a stop over.

destroyed 28 bridges and 93 houses in their path. No less than 34 people perished in one night. In earlier times Lynmouth was better known for its association with literary figures such as Southey and Shelley.

Lynton situated on its hill high above Lynmouth can be reached by a cliff railway propelled by water built in 1815 the gift to Lynton of Sir George Newnes the publisher. Of course no purist walker would even consider using this! Beyond Lynton is one of the finest stretches of the path so far, the North Walk, a feat of Victorian ingenuity, tarmac it is true but a great walk so high above the sea. Often along this path you may see a herd of feral goats; locally they are often the source of dissension. The local gardeners hate them as they munch their way through hard sown rows of peas; the tourist-minded welcome them as an unusual attraction. Mind you, even the most avid visitor will regret getting down wind of a billy-goat in the height of summer.

The Heddon's Mouth valley is a delightful place with a limekiln at the seaward end and a public house, the Hunter's Inn, at the other. The highest point of the path is reached at the Great Hangman and legends abound of sheep-stealers being deservedly hanged here. More prosaically 'hang' is a slope, and 'man' (similar to 'mine' in Minehead), is from the

The coast path winds past Foreland Point, Devon's furthest north, just east of Lynton. The lighthouse is now automated and the National Trust rent out the former keeper's cottage. Below: an aerial view of Lynmouth.

13

Celtic for a stone outcrop or hill. The view surprisingly is even better from the Little Hangman below, where you can look across Combe Martin Bay. Nearby silver-lead mines were active intermittently for about six hundred years and some of the silver was made into regalia, now in the Exeter Guildhall. Combe Martin has a winding main street two miles long, claimed to be the longest in England. Well back from the shore is the Pack of Cards Inn dating from the eighteenth century. Its features are based on the numbers significant to a pack of cards; it has four floors to represent the four suits, and fifty-two windows the number of cards in a pack. It was built as a private house, reputedly by a successful gambler. Strange as it may seem even when it became an inn for a long while it was not called the Pack of Cards.

Beyond Combe Martin, at Watermouth, wartime trials were held for PLUTO the Pipe Line Under The Ocean that was used so effectively after D-Day in the World War II to get fuel to our forces in France.

The first view of Ilfracombe is from Hillsborough, the big hill just to the east of it. Originally Ilfracombe was a small market town and fishing port; over the years it developed into a small trading port and later still, from the Napoleonic period, as a resort. The Rev. John Swete's one comment on Ilfracombe's tourist business was to express

The bottom of the Lynton to Lynmouth Cliff Railway at Lynmouth. Sir George Newnes the publisher funded it.

Right: Formerly the Kings Arms Hotel, seen here c.1900, the Pack of Cards was said to have been built using money won in a card game by Squire George Ley who died in 1716.

his disappointment that there was only one bathing machine! This tourist development occurred much later than that of South Devon because communications were so much worse. Arguments of exclusivity as against numbers, though, came early to the town when steamers started to bring in hard-drinking Welsh miners.

The descent into the town takes you past Rapparee Cove where the slave ship *London* went ashore in a gale in 1796 with the loss of life of at least sixty slaves. Yellow pebbles, used as ballast in the ship, and the remains of iron fetters have been found on the beach. The ship had been lying off the port when the gale was forecast. The captain refused to take refuge, and it is assumed this was because he knew that if he went into harbour a previous legal judgement had ruled the all slaves must be freed.

Ilfracombe is a departure point for Lundy Island. Before leaving the town all walkers will have the opportunity of making their own judgement on the recently built Landmark Theatre. Is it worthy of its award as an architectural triumph? Alternatively should it ever have been built in that setting?

A few miles along the coast from Ilfracombe is Bull Point lighthouse. The original tower was built in 1879 but it

Looking east over Combe Martin Bay. The land rises behind to the Little Hangman and then Great Hangman at 1045 feet (328 meters), the highest point on the whole path.

The Landmark Theatre has drawn much controversy over its design.

Originally built in 1879, Bull Point lighthouse was rebuilt in 1972 on a nearby site.

The lower reaches of the River Taw, on the left Crow Point, in front of Braunton Burrows, behind them the town of Braunton itself. Braunton Burrows is now a Biosphere Reserve important for its range of plants.

suffered from a landslip and needed to be moved and rebuilt in 1972. Later, one reaches Morte Point. This sounds a gloomy place, and could it is true refer to death, but it could also derive from an early word meaning 'short and stubby'. Barricane Beach just before Woolacombe is known to locals as the 'Shell Beach' for obvious reasons. Woolacombe developed as an Edwardian seaside resort and has become very popular again with the increased interest in surfing.

Baggy Point is an exceptional viewpoint for the surrounding coastline of Barnstaple (or Bideford Bay). Both names seem to be used by locals, so if they can not decide, maybe others should keep out of the argument! Rocket apparatus training posts, for life saving at sea, were once a common sight all round the South Western peninsula, now they are relatively rare but one intact post remains on Baggy Point.

Braunton Burrows is the largest sand dune system in the United Kingdom and has recently acquired designation as a Biosphere Reserve. The name 'burrows' originates from the large population of rabbits. In times past a train load of rabbits was sent weekly to Covent Garden market. American forces used the Burrows as a training area in World War II and occupied the Saunton Sands Hotel as an officer's mess. The main route north from Bideford long ago was very different from that today. In the seventeenth century, it used to be by land to Appledore, then by ferry across the mouths of the Torridge and Taw to near Crow Point, finally continuing by land again to Braunton.

The last leg of the path in this section is generally eastwards, and from Braunton on makes use of the old Barnstaple-to-Ilfracombe railway line, passing the airbase at Chivenor. You need to be on your guard against speeding cyclists, some of whom seem to treat the route as a speedway. There is in fact no need now to go right into Barnstaple, unless you are looking for refreshment or bed and board, since the new 'Downstream Bridge', now called 'Taw Bridge', part of the town's western by-pass opened in 2006.

Croyde Bay with Croyde Village behind it has prospered with the increase in surfing.

SUGGESTIONS FOR SHORT WALKS

Lynton – North Walk

For those who appreciate a short but stunning high level walk above the sea there is a very good stretch at Lynton. In Lynton, walk up the main street Lee Road to take the minor road Longmead to the Valley of Rocks. This is a road but by using pavements and verges you can avoid the road itself. This soon becomes attractive in itself, especially if a cricket match should be in progress in this natural amphitheater. At the turning circle towards the end of the valley, below the impressive pile of Castle Rock, turn right to pick up the well-signed Coast Path and go back along the North Walk, as it is called, towards Lynton. Ignore the sign that says Lynton via Hollerday Hill. (If it is a clear day not only will you have superb views across the

The path across the bottom of the picture is the North Walk at Lynton, part of the Coast Path and certainly one of its highlights. The rocky formations such as the one right give the name to the valley behind – Valley of Rocks.

Bristol Channel to South Wales but also ahead to Foreland Point Lighthouse). The path goes over the Cliff Railway and very shortly there is a fork left to Lynmouth but you want right to Lynton, go up the slope and you are back in the main street, just above the church. There is a tea garden in the Valley of Rocks and plenty of refreshment in Lynton. The circuit is under 2½ miles (4 km).

A close up view of Castle Rock in the Valley of Rocks. There is another similar named valley on the Coast Path but it is far away at Watcombe outside Torquay in South Devon.

Croyde Bay – Baggy Point

Park at the National Trust car park Croyde Bay 432 397. The footpath you require leaves by a stile from the north east corner of the car park, signed 'Middleborough Hill'. The path goes steeply up the field to join a hedged path. Presently there is a sign 'Viewpoint' follow this. Then close to top there is a sign left to 'Viewpoint', you may wish to explore but the path you need is right 'Baggy Point'. Cross a field, to the corner of a wall where there is a sign pointing back 'NT Car Park'. Continue along the wall down into the dip and up the other side. At the top of the next field there is a waymark pointing left follow this. At the end of the field is a stile cross over and turn right keeping close to the wall, cross another stile still keeping wall/bank on right. (As you near top of rise, view forward to Morte Point and Woolacombe opens up). Go over one more stile to bear left to

Looking south across Baggy Point towards Croyde Bay, in the distance is the north Devon coast from Westward Ho! stretching out to Clovelly and Hartland Point.

join in a few yards the Coast Path, continue to Baggy Point. Here be careful, it is easy to miss the true Coast and best path onwards. As you round corner there is ahead a tall rocket-practice pole with steps each side, walk towards this then in same direction to rail fence. Follow this fence down past a seat and through a small gate. The path descends steeply then turns sharp left. (There is a wide sweep of view from Baggy Point taking in the Taw/Torridge estuary, Westward Ho! the stretch of coast past Buck's Mills, Clovelly and out towards Hartland Point not to mention Lundy Island seaward). Return along the Coast Path, passing a tea garden to the car park. Just about 3 miles 4.8 km).

Below: Launching Braunton lifeboat at Saunton in 1904.

CHAPTER 2
BARNSTAPLE TO BUDE

The route is back along the south of the Taw estuary, after that it proceeds up the Torridge as far as Bideford and back down its western side to Appledore. From here it travels westward past Westward Ho! and Clovelly to turn sharply south at Hartland Point to continue to Bude in Cornwall.

This section is a mixture, walking the estuaries is easy and some find this a refreshing change. From Westward Ho! onwards more energy is required but the route is undoubtedly scenic and there is much of interest. The North Devon section running south from Hartland Point is often called 'The Iron Coast', this is no misnomer, the scenery is highly dramatic, and some might call it severe. However, many will tell you it is the best stretch of the entire Coast Path. Walkers are warned that the final leg, Hartland Quay to Bude, has been regarded as the toughest stretch of the whole path!

As previously said, thanks to the Downstream Bridge, there is no need to go into the town of Barnstaple now, if you want to just walk briskly from say Braunton to Bideford. However, you will miss much if you do bypass the place. This is because, not only does it offer plenty of refreshment and accommodation, it is also a place of great antiquity and has much of interest.

Looking west from the mouth of the Taw/Torridge. In the foreground is Appledore; behind left is Northam and behind right, on the coast, is Westward Ho! Appledore has a long history of shipbuilding and the occupation still continues. Westward Ho! is remembered because it was so named after Rudyard Kipling's book. He spent his schooldays here.

Historically Barnstaple goes back over a thousand years to its foundation as a Saxon *burgh*, though it is only right to point out that the original settlement was at Pilton, now a suburb. There was a Norman Castle and later the town was walled. It had a market and was for centuries an important trading port. Irish wool was for many years the staple import but Daniel Defoe wrote of ships despatched to Warrington on the River Mersey to fetch rock salt that was used to cure the local herring catch. The first record of a bridge here is 1312. However this particular record refers to the appointment of a priest to the chapel on the bridge, and this leads to the suspicion that the bridge is older than that date.

Looking west from the mouth of the Rivers Taw and Torridge. Crow Point on the right, the spur of land beyond the river is Northam Burrows and in the distance is Hartland Point. Northam Burrows is now a Countryside Park. In years gone by the pot-wallopers of Northam used to gather every Whit-Monday to collect up pebbles.

Below: Butcher's Row in Barnstaple c.1900.

There is not space here to describe everything that is of interest in the town so two items will have to suffice. In The Bank, a restaurant in Boutport Street, there is a wonderful plaster moulded ceiling dating probably from Tudor times. Look particularly for the elephant, as undoubtedly the master craftsman who completed the work had never seen one but had relied on travellers' tales as to how it looked! The other feature is Butcher's Row a minor street running from the High Street to Boutport Street. It is a street reminiscent of eastern bazaars or medieval streets, where similar craftsman worked cheek by jowl. In fact it does not go back to the Middle Ages but only to Victorian times and was set up in response to a cholera outbreak. Nonetheless it is probably unique in England.

Bideford Quay and bridge, c.1900. Bideford bridge is noted for its 24 arches of different widths, once thought to have been due to varying sums given by rich merchants for its foundation, but now known to correspond to the size of the timbers of the original wooden bridge.

Summertime at Instow once posed a dilemma for walkers; take the ferry that ran across to Appledore, or walk both sides of the Torridge estuary through Bideford. Unfortunately it now seems that the ferry is discontinued so there will be only one option. Although Instow was the first North Devon resort to be connected in succession by turnpike road and rail, it never achieved greatness. It has a preserved box to remind one of days gone by and the green livery denotes it once belonged to the Southern Railway.

According to W.G. Hoskins, the historian, Bideford 'is the most attractive town in North Devon. Just as at Barnstaple there is an ancient bridge, although the town's very name reveals the bridge was a later convenience! For many years it was a rival to the port of Barnstaple and although at first it was relatively insignificant, as the Taw silted up Bideford increased in importance from the sixteenth century onwards. It imported wool, had a sizeable share in the Newfoundland trade and a large trade with Virginia and Maryland, bringing in quantities of tobacco. All

Engineers and railwaymen pose alongside the steam locomotive 'Creedy' which was the first train to arrive at Bideford's old Cross Park station in October 1855.

21

these trades gradually declined but from 1830 onwards a considerable emigrant traffic to America developed. Today the last steady bulk trade is the shipping out of ball-clay from the North Devon beds.

Appledore was probably the Tawmouth of ancient times. It has a long history of fishing, shipping and, indeed, shipbuilding. This is carried on at the massive undercover shipyard which employs several hundreds building dredgers, tugs, tankers and even a research ship. There was once another yard that specialized in replicas making amongst other things, a Roman galley, a Viking ship, and the *Golden Hind*. Appledore was well known for its schooners in days gone by and claims to be the last place in England to make its 'living' by sail. There is an interesting Maritime Museum run by the North Devon Trust in Odun House. The port has had a very long history of involvement in the herring fishing industry, but the humble herring was not the only fish caught from Appledore. The Torridge and Taw were salmon rivers of considerable importance. Licensed fishermen in special salmon boats still net in their assigned stretches, or drifts as they are called. The involvement in the Newfoundland trade is evidenced by The Beaver Inn. It may be of interest too, in these days of less formal dress, that Appledore once made gloves and indeed had a collar factory.

Seafaring and shipbuilding were the principal trades of the North Devon ports and few knew better the dangers of those coastal waters than the captains of local vessels.

Most grandparents are pleased to see their grandchildren but often relieved to see them go again. Have sympathy for those of times gone by in Appledore. Each year in spring shipbuilders used to go to New England, because of plentiful timber there, build a ship sail her back under jury (makeshift) rig to finish her at Appledore over the winter. After a few years roughing it the men decided they were missing out on well-cooked meals so started to take some of their wives with them. This meant the grandparents had a very long 'baby sit'!

Behind the pebble ridges in what is now the Northam Countryside Park the pot-wallopers (householders) of Northam used to assemble every Whit Monday to gather up and return as many pebbles as possible back to the sea, thus improving their grazing land. Westward Ho! itself claims exclusivity as being the only town called after a book. It was a late holiday resort that used the title of Charles Kingsley's

Lying between Appledore and Westward Ho!, the village of Northam, seen here in Victorian times, is said to have been the site of a battle between the Danes and Alfred the Great.

book. Another literary connection is that Rudyard Kipling went to school here and his *Stalky & Co* is based on his adventures with his schoolmates.

Just west of Westward Ho! the Coast Path makes use of part of the track of the Bideford–Westward Ho!–Appledore railway. This was a very short-lived affair; the first part from Bideford to Appledore opened in 1901, the remainder to Appledore in 1908. The line closed in 1917 so it was only fully operational for nine years. The loco was sent off for war service in France on tracks specially laid for the purpose on Bideford road bridge.

At Abbotsham Cliffs can be found the other end of the thin coal seam from Bideford; this fuel was used to fire the local limekilns. Abbotsham takes it name from the fact it once belonged to Tavistock Abbey. The village lies a mile off the path and was in the news in 2001. A builder carrying out renovations found a hoard of coins hidden in a pottery container. There were 435 coins, including Spanish and Irish but mostly English. The earliest were from Tudor times and the latest one of the Commonwealth, 1653. The main mystery, and one we are not likely to solve, is why the hoard was hidden. It may not have been hidden exactly in 1653, but it is likely to have been fairly soon after. The second Civil War had come and gone. We

Published in 1855, Rudyard Kipling's Westward Ho! gave it's name to the present seaside village.

23

were fighting the Dutch at the time but this was principally a maritime affair off England's south-east coast. So why were they hidden? Might it have been a domestic affair? There is a good display concerning the hoard in the museum section of the Burton Art Gallery in Bideford. This is only yards from the Coast Path in Bideford.

If there was no Clovelly then surely Buck's Mills would be better known! It is an attractive and interesting place but is little regarded compared to its nearby neighbour. Richard Cole, who built the first harbour here, is one of the contenders for being 'Old King Cole'. Be that as it may there was a small port here for many years. Lundy's corn was brought in to be milled; limestone came from Caldy Island off the Welsh coast to be burnt for lime. The massive inclined plane attests this past activity. In such an isolated place inter-marriage was common and over the years the surname of the majority of the populace became Braund. A plaque set up here is a reminder of this fact.

Above: Clovelly 1900. Below: A bird's eye view of the narrow cobbled street that runs through Clovelly's tightly packed cottages down to the harbour.

Clovelly is approached along its Hobby Drive. The village has been well described as being like a waterfall, its 650 steps taking the place of a street. Sledges and donkeys are still used to carry goods. It was once chiefly known as a herring

port, having over 60 boats in the trade. Later the
Hamlyns, the London banking family,
bought the estate, from the Cary family,
and thankfully preserved it. The
portrait of Christina Hamlyn who
famously said, "I dwell among
mine own people" hangs in the
dining room of The New Inn.
Charles Kingsley's father, who
was also named Charles, was the
incumbent here.

Mouth Mill is an isolated and
beautiful stream outlet a little
west of Clovelly. It has, on its
boulder beach, an impressive natu-
rally-formed multi-arch rock formation called Blackchurch Rock. Shipload
Bay was the site for the original cable
carrying power to Lundy. On a hot day a swim
seems very inviting and getting down to the beach is no
problem. However, after your swim by the time you have
regained the Coast Path you are as warm as you were before

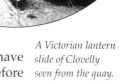

A Victorian lantern slide of Clovelly seen from the quay.

The main street at Clovelly is all cobblestones and shallow steps. Goods are brought down on sledges. Someone once described the village as being like a waterfall tumbling down the hill. Here is an aerial view of the quay at Clovelly, note the lifeboat house slipway. The official RNLI lifeboat is now at Appledore, but the village maintains its own lifeboat.

The coastline west of Clovelly is so tree covered in many places, that although you are walking on cliff tops, you do not always get the views you might expect. There are however surprise lookout points that compensate.

you descended! Next, you come to Barley Bay. The car park from which the road to the lighthouse used to descend has now partly subsided. As the path leaves the road there is a catchment area which used to collect rainwater for use in the lighthouse. Trinity House, the organisation that oversees lighthouses and pilotage, built the lighthouse in 1874; Bishop Temple of Exeter who later became Archbishop of Canterbury blessed it. Hartland Point is probably the 'Hercules promontory' of the ancient geographer Ptolemy.

This is the closest point on the mainland to Lundy, about twelve miles away, so take the opportunity if visibility is good to have a look at it. The name derives from the Norsk *Lundi*, meaning isle of puffins, and is one of only two Norsk names to appear in Devon. In the nineteenth century it was for a while jokingly referred to as the 'Kingdom of Heaven', the proprietor then being a Reverend W. H. Heaven.

The coastline south from Hartland Point is so rugged and at times so awe-inspiring that it is difficult to do it justice with mere words. The contorted rock strata, bent and twisted by geological upheavals, has since been hammered by ferocious seas, leaving this most impressive coastal scenery. An additional delight to the eye is provided by a series of coastal waterfalls. These occur where the power of the sea is so great that it has cut through into a stream valley, shortening the stream, and making a waterfall. The first fine example of this

is Titchberry Water and the Smoothlands Valley. The valley, though substantial, contains only the merest trickle of a stream. Here the sea has broken through into the course of Titchberry Water, that once ran down the Smoothlands Valley, creating a waterfall further north-east. There is another waterfall at Blegberry Water and several more south of Hartland Quay that were created in the same way.

Damehole Point is a dramatic headland and has arguably the most exciting right of way in England going out on to it.

Looking east along the coast from Hartland Point. To the left of the lighthouse is Barley Bay. Behind is the 'golf-ball' of the radar station.

Left: Looking south from Hartland Point down what has been aptly named the 'iron coast'. The second headland from the lighthouse is Damehole Point. There is a footpath leading out to this superb viewpoint. The road running down to the lighthouse has become unsafe due to the action of the sea.

Hartland Quay – the name has stayed but the quay itself has long gone, pounded by the Atlantic Ocean. The small house to the left of the road on the cliff top was a 'Rocket House' where life-saving rockets were stored for use along this dangerous coast. The Coastal Footpath is at its best both north and south of Hartland Quay.

A rocket crew on the Devon coast practising the launch of a Breeches buoy c.1930. This apparatus was used to fire a rope across to a stricken ship in order to bring shipwrecked crew and passengers safely to shore.

There are many though who will opt not to exercise their right! Blackpool Mill was altered to become the Devonshire home of the Dashwood family in a television costume drama *Sense and Sensibility* by Jane Austen. On the Warren Cliff is a tower that was probably a summerhouse, but one almost certainly built for visual effect, a folly, for the nearby stately home, Hartland Abbey. There had originally been a religious foundation here set up in the eleventh century by Gytha, the wife of Earl Godwin, as thanks for his rescue from shipwreck. She was pleased to have him back!

Just before the descent to Hartland Quay is the Rocket House, once used for storing the life-saving gear that had much use on this severe coast. Hartland Quay itself not only has dramatic scenery but also has an interesting history. There was a small harbour here from the reign of Elizabeth I

until the late nineteenth century. Hence the 'Quay' in the name. A gale in 1887 partly destroyed the pier and it was completely destroyed in another gale in 1896. Mixed cargoes were brought ashore, including glass from Sunderland and lead for the repair of Hartland Church. There were at one time, three limekilns and a malt house. The commerce was enough to warrant a small bank that issued £1 and £5 notes until 1833. Maybe it was thirst caused by the limekilns but it is on record that the inn was closed in 1874 because of excessive drinking.

Shortly after leaving Hartland Quay the Coast Path passes through a grassy valley behind St Catherine's Tor, a pointed cliff top. The valley was once the site of a swan pool for Hartland Abbey, in the days when swan was on the menu! The cliff is called St Catherine's because there was a medieval chapel dedicated to her on the top. Until quite recently floor tiles from the chapel could be picked up on the beach below. There was a collection in the old Bideford Museum, unfortunately now lost. Shortly afterwards comes the valley called Speke's Mill Mouth. Here there is a dramatic 50-foot plus waterfall cascading down the rock face. When the stream levels are high enough you are rewarded with twin falls. This is certainly quite the most spectacular waterfall anywhere on the Coast Path.

There were a series of shipwrecks near Longpeak, from the *Reine Leonie* in 1879 to *Goliath* in 1969. Perhaps the most

The beach left centre of the picture is Welcombe Mouth and the stream which flows into the sea here has the delightful name of Strawberry Water. The beach to the extreme right of the picture is Marsland Mouth it is here that walkers can cross into Cornwall on a little wooden bridge.

Litter Mouth, North Cornwall, has one of a series of waterfalls to be found along this coast. The cliff to the right of the picture is Cornakey Cliff.

The extraordinary Reverend Hawker of Morwenstow at the vicarage door.

dramatic rescue occurred when the *Green Ranger,* a Royal Fleet Auxiliary Tanker under tow, broke loose and went aground just south of Longpeak. Helicopters, rocket apparatus and lifeboats were all involved in the attempts at rescue, and eventually all seven members of the crew were safely brought ashore by breeches buoy. (Royal Fleet Auxiliary vessels were ships that assisted Royal Navy operations but flew a Blue flag rather than the White Ensign).

At Embury Beacon there was an Iron Age settlement. Unfortunately the cliffs are so soft that every year more of it falls into the sea. It was excavated in 1973 and some pottery was found. It was also established that there was a surrounding rampart and ditch and that the people inside lived in wooden huts with shelters for their animals. After Welcombe on the descent to Marsland Mouth there is a little stone hut once used by the author Ronald Duncan; it has been left as a shelter facility for walkers. At Marsland Mouth itself is the border between North Devon and Cornwall. It is only four miles from the source of the river Tamar that flows south to form the border between Cornwall and Devon.

There is a long climb up to Henna Cliff, just over 450 feet high, which is the second highest sheer drop of any English cliff, only Beachy Head exceeds it. You descend close to the site of St Morwenna's Well but do not dally looking for it, because it fell victim to the encroaching sea. Morwenstow is close inland. It is not on the Coast Path but many will go there for refreshment or lodging. It is well known as being the parish of the eccentric cleric the Revd R. S. Hawker. He encouraged animals to come to church but once excommunicated a cat that caught a mouse during divine service! He is best known for starting harvest festival services and writing *And Shall Trelawney Die,* an unofficial Cornish national anthem. Hawker's hut is only a few yards off the path above Lucky Hole. The locals though were not always complimentary about Hawker's habits. They said that he so seldom took a bath that when he did the seawater was dirty all the way to Bude!

At Lower Sharpnose Point you cannot miss what used to be RAF Cleave Camp but is now Composite Signals Organisation Station (CSOS), a satellite tracking station. There is

Lower Sharpnose Point, with the Composite Signal Organisation Station, Morwenstow. This used to be Cleave Camp, an RAF establishment.

then a long descent to Duckpool in the Coombe Valley. Upstream from here was Stow Barton, the great mansion of the famous Grenville family: Roger Grenville captained the *Mary Rose*, Sir Richard the *Revenge*, Bevil died leading his Cornishmen at the battle of Landsdowne Hill in the Civil War, and John was handsomely rewarded for aiding the Restoration.

At Crooklets, in the guise of a rash of beach huts, civilisation suddenly thrusts itself forward, and the immediate reaction is to wonder if one really cares all that much for civilisation. Probably this is a thought that has occurred to many a walker returning from quieter regions, until, of course, the prospect of a hot bath and a cooked meal destroys such finer feelings!

SUGGESTIONS FOR SHORT WALKS

Clovelly
From the main car park go down towards the village but turn left along the road that at that point also serves as the Coast Path, signed Coast Path Brownsham. Then follow Coast Path signs. You soon leave the road through a high gate into a field. Follow the track forking slightly right, presently you go down steps through a rhododendron shrubbery. And come

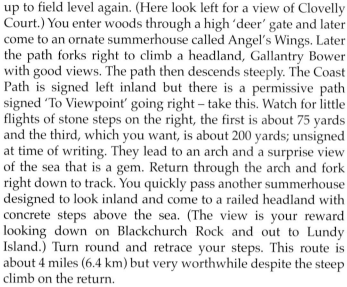

up to field level again. (Here look left for a view of Clovelly Court.) You enter woods through a high 'deer' gate and later come to an ornate summerhouse called Angel's Wings. Later the path forks right to climb a headland, Gallantry Bower with good views. The path then descends steeply. The Coast Path is signed left inland but there is a permissive path signed 'To Viewpoint' going right – take this. Watch for little flights of stone steps on the right, the first is about 75 yards and the third, which you want, is about 200 yards; unsigned at time of writing. They lead to an arch and a surprise view of the sea that is a gem. Return through the arch and fork right down to track. You quickly pass another summerhouse designed to look inland and come to a railed headland with concrete steps above the sea. (The view is your reward looking down on Blackchurch Rock and out to Lundy Island.) Turn round and retrace your steps. This route is about 4 miles (6.4 km) but very worthwhile despite the steep climb on the return.

Northcott Mouth a little north of Bude. The village of Poughill, pronounced 'Puffill' is in the middle distance.

Hartland Quay

A splendid walk that is short but not without exertion is south from Hartland Quay. Park in the car park 223 246 there and follow the Coast Path south signed Speke's Mill. You pass a series of sea-captures*, go behind St Catherine's Tor. (There was once a chapel on the top of the Tor and a pool for swans where you walk.) Cross the stream go through a meadow and ascend the other side, and then drop steeply to the waterfalls at Speke's Mill Mouth. They are the best falls that the Coast Path can offer; you may need to remind yourself of that as you climb back up the last hill you came down! (There is a path down to the beach and the bottom of the falls if you want an extension.) Distance is 2 miles (3.2 km) but it may seem more.

Crooklets Beach at Bude. Bude is the first sizeable urban area on the coast in over twenty miles. Bude was originally called Bede then more often Bude Haven.

*Streams normally cut down to sea-level at their mouths. A sea-capture, and therefore a waterfall, occurs when the sea erodes in from the coast and cuts into a stream valley higher up its course.

CHAPTER 3
BUDE TO NEWQUAY

For the whole of this chapter the route is approximately south-west. Passing Crackington Haven, Boscastle, Tintagel and as far as Port Isaac the path continues in rugged vein. After that it softens somewhat, crossing the River Camel to Padstow, and so on to Newquay. Pentire Point on the north side of the Camel estuary is considered by some to provide the finest all round view in Cornwall.

Because of the lack of accommodation nearby most walkers will call a halt in Bude, even if they are not using it as a major staging post. There are two ways of looking at the town. Pevsner wrote 'not an attractive harbour-town compared with others in Cornwall and Devon.' Sean Jennett went on the record 'it (Bude) had the good fortune to grow up well back from the sea, along the margins of open downs called Summerleaze, with the result that the beaches are everywhere backed by downland.' Therefore you can decide

Looking north from Bude, CSOS Morwenstow can just be seen on the coast towards the top of the picture. Bude Canal towards the left of the picture, the River Neet towards the right. Bude has connections with Sir Goldsworthy Gurney the prolific inventor.

Bude canal took fifty years to build but the engineering ideas were ahead of their time so that it was never a great commercial success.

Small coastal trading vessels lie in the canal basin at Bude in the 1880s.

with which writer you agree – but maybe you should not decide until you have at least seen the rest of the North Coast of Cornwall.

Originally called Bede or more often Bude Haven, Bude was a late developing resort but similarly to a number of other places on the Atlantic coast it has grown in popularity with the increase in surfing. It has two major interesting historical connections: the canal and associations with Sir Goldsworthy Gurney. Canals, whilst not as scarce as hen's teeth, are not common in Cornwall. Financially, the Bude Canal was never a success and from that angle it is a pity that its long protracted gestation ever gave birth; its first enactment was in 1774 and it opened in 1825. From the enthusiast's angle it is very interesting. It was built to include no less than six inclined planes. These were the ramps up which the barges were hauled to avoid making a

series of locks. The barges on the Bude Canal were unusual having wheels attached to their outsides so that they could be hauled up or let down the slopes. Unfortunately, the engineering was ahead of its time and paid the price with unreliability of operation. The canal was built chiefly to carry sand from the beaches, taking it inland to act as a fertilizer for the fields, although other items also were carried.

Sir Goldsworthy Gurney (1793-1875) the Cornish inventor was a versatile multi-talented, surgeon and engineer. He was born near Padstow and lived the last part of his life at Poughill (pronounced 'Puffil') near Bude. He is remembered for his invention of a steam-carriage, and his advances in ventilating and lighting used in the House of Commons. One of his lighting innovations was called Bude Light. However, he is chiefly remembered in Bude for Bude Castle, not a castle but council offices. It was built by the ingenious Gurney to prove that houses could be built on foundations comprising a concrete raft.

An 1827 print showing Gurney's steam carriage in action.

Worth noting in Bude is the plinth above Summerlease Beach that is inscribed 'This Monument commemorates the hospitality of Bude to Clifton College in the war years 1941–1945'. A nice way to say thank you. It displays the distance to some places walkers are likely to visit and some they are not, for instance the North Pole!

Efford Beacon is a good place to look around and look ahead. If the weather is fine it is possible to see to the south-

The Temple of the Four Winds, locally known as the 'Pepper Pot' on Efford Down south of Bude. It had to be moved because the sea was undermining it but it was re-erected out of true.

Widmouth Bay south of Bude. The growth of surfing as a leisure activity has favoured a number of places like this along the Atlantic coastline.

Walkers have had an easy passage through the Bude area but now start to meet sterner stuff again over the Dizzard Point.

east the loftiest tors of Dartmoor, Yes Tor and High Willhays, at just over two thousand feet the highest land in the south of England. Looking down along the coast is the sharp outline of Cambeak just beyond Crackington Haven. The second and intrusive squat outline is the big hotel at Tintagel, and in the distance is the headland of Trevose, some twenty-eight miles away. It is worth making a short diversion on to the beach at Millook to see the contorted strata on the northern side. It is such a good example that pictures of it have been used in textbooks. There were plans in 1835 to bring a railway here and develop the place into a port called Melluach. As you can easily gather, the scheme, like so many others of this type came to nothing.

Crackington Haven has grown recently but once it was a quieter rural place as the old donkey shoes that are occasionally found, bear testimony. It was though, in addition, a very small port exporting the local slate and importing coal. Land here was donated to the National Trust in memory of those killed in the Battle of Britain.

After Crackington Haven you have the long climb up behind Cambeak to the top of High Cliff. This is the highest point you will reach in Cornwall at 731feet (223m), and though the cliff is nothing like a sheer drop it is a most rewarding view. As a young architect Thomas Hardy was sent to restore St Juliot church up in the Valency Valley behind Boscastle. Whilst there he also wrote *A Pair of Blue Eyes* in which he used the cliff top as a setting for a dramatic – and romantic – cliff top rescue. Hardy was obviously not one to waste his spare time because, apart from the restoration work and the writing, he also courted the vicar's sister-in-law, Emma Gifford, who became his first wife!

Crackington Haven, Pencarrow Point to the left of the picture. Just as they did at Boscastle in 2004, heavy rains then flooding caused problems at Crackington Haven.

Though there is much good scenery on this section there is no doubt that Pentargon is the jewel. Unfortunately when making a new path – the old had been undermined by action of the sea – it was moved further inland than was needed. This means you do not easily get the view you should of the dramatic waterfall. Another impressive natural feature is the blowhole as you reach the Boscastle inlet. This is at the right-angled bend of the northern limb of Boscastle Harbour. If the tide is right and a good sea running this can look and indeed sound dramatic. The sea outside is driven through a rapidly diminishing cave that has a small escape hole into the harbour itself. It is well worth walking many a mile to see this at its best.

Boscastle has a long history, but it was as a port that the place developed. Looking at the narrow, sinuous entrance this may be hard to believe, but natural harbours are scarce on the north Cornish coast so even places more unlikely than Boscastle were used as ports. Cargoes of beer, salt, coal, bricks and limestone arrived here; minerals and corn went out. However, it was the rise of the slate trade in the nineteenth century that really made the place busy. This applied all down the coast here in places such as Port William, Port Gaverne, Port Isaac etc. not to mention smaller inlets and even loading on beaches.

Fore Street, Boscastle, 1905.

Sir Richard Grenville built the inner jetty in the harbour in 1584, when he lived at Stowe Barton north of Bude. The outer jetty, which was built about two hundred years later, had a more eventful history. It was blown up by a mine in World War II. The National Trust repaired it in 1962 with granite brought from the old Laira Bridge at Plymouth. Boscastle is also known for being one of the last places where horse-drawn coaches ran. A regular service continued up until the early 1920s. More recently Boscastle is remembered for its flood in 2004. This occurred in August similar to the one at Lynmouth, both floods caused by torrential rain. Though enormous damage was done to Boscastle, unlike Lynmouth there was not a single casualty. Partly this was due to the good fortune that the peak came in daylight, not at night, as well as more modern rescue techniques such as the use of helicopters.

If you wish to see the Maze Carvings, you must make a short diversion up Rocky Valley. For a long time these were considered to be of the Bronze Age, say three thousand five hundred years old. That being so, one is surprised they have survived. Unfortunately more recently it has been suggested they could be a Victorian fake, let us hope that this is not so!

Boscastle with its sinuous harbour. Access was always difficult but local competition was scarce so it became a busy port. The outer breakwater had an argument with a mine, the explosive sort, in World War II and had to be rebuilt.

Lye Rock, nearly an islet off the headland Willapark. This was the scene of a dramatic rescue in a blizzard in 1893 of the crew of an Italian vessel Iota. The poor cabin boy who did not survive is buried in Tintagel churchyard.

Beyond Bossiney Haven look for Lye Rock to seaward; this was the scene of a desperate rescue in a blizzard in 1893. A small Italian vessel the *Iota* was wrecked there, but by heroic efforts local rescuers saved all but one of the crew. He was Catanese Domenico, a fourteen-year-old cabin boy. His grave is in Tintagel's churchyard, along with a bare wooden cross and a lifebelt from the *Iota*. What might have saved life marks his death. Bossiney itself was obviously once a place of more importance than it is now because it sent two MPs to Parliament. At one time one of these was Sir Francis Drake, no less. However, as the centuries passed it became notorious as one of the most rotten of the 'Rotten Boroughs', one man electing both MPs!

The last headland before Tintagel is Barras Nose. It was purchased by the National Trust in 1897 two years after their formation and became their first coastal holding. There were plans afoot to build a hotel on it; the purchase prevented this happening. The good news for the walker, particularly one with a discerning mind, is that you do not have to go into the tourist trap of King Arthur wonderland in the town above, as you can walk by underneath. It is amazing how much myth, story and legend has grown up on the most tenuous factual basis. There may have been a Celtic chieftain who could be represented as Arthur, but if there was he certainly was not wearing the medieval armour and accoutrements as depicted in picture books!

If you opt out of the town you still pass the castle and the church. The castle site has a very long history but not always as a castle. It was once a Celtic monastery, though this had gone before the Norman Conquest. The castle was possibly built in the 11th century by Reginald Earl of Cornwall, more certainly a hundred years later it was rebuilt and extended by Earl Richard. Despite its dramatic appearance its history is mundane. It never saw a shot fired in anger but did for a while serve as a prison. The church St Matriana is older than the castle and is certainly Norman, although Pevsner credits it with some Saxon features. It claims to be the oldest church in Cornwall in regular use and inside has a tranquility all its own.

If you opt for the town see the Old Post Office, so called because it was from 1844 to 1892 the letter receiving office. It

Tintagel with the so-called 'Island' in the foreground. Originally there was a Celtic monastery on the summit, later a castle which never saw a shot fired in anger. The large building on the mainland is the Camelot Castle Hotel.

*Tintagel village
c.1900 looking west
along the main
street. The Old
Post Office is on the
left, now a National
Trust property.*

*The Island,
Tintagel, clearly
showing the outline
of early settlement
and, at the land-
ward end, the
remains of the castle
Inner Ward.*

was sold, fortunately, to folk with preservation in mind, and later was acquired by the National Trust. As a building it pre-dates by centuries its use as a post office. It is really a fourteenth century building in the style of a medieval manor house. The Wharncliffe Arms Hotel is named after the Wharncliffes who were at one time the most important land owning family in Tintagel. In front of the hotel is a much-battered ancient stone cross. Its dedication, translated from the Latin, reads 'Aelnat made this cross for the sake of his soul'. We know that the cross was once used as a gatepost.

We also know that Aelnat was a Saxon name, but apart from that we can only conjecture about something much older than the Old Post Office.

Tintagel may or may not have any connection with a mythical King Arthur but it certainly does with custard! Eirenkon was the home of F. T. Glasscock, a man who made a fortune out of custard. Older readers may remember 'Monk and Glass custard'. He came to Tintagel to retire but became much involved in the modern promotion of King Arthur. Like other men of wealth before him his hobby proved extremely lucrative, in fact it laid the foundations of a second fortune. He died in 1934, on his way to America on the old Cunard liner *Queen Mary*, being buried at sea.

Soon after leaving Tintagel Church behind you become aware of the nearby slate quarries, and there is a particularly spectacular rock pillar left in one quarry behind Hole Beach. Some of these quarries were still used within living memory. The work was incredibly hard and in places shifts had to coincide with the tides, sometimes starting at four in the morning! Before descending to Trebarwith, look inland, for in one of the three slate quarries at Trewarmett, called the Prince of Wales, there is a ruined engine house. Later there are dozens along the path, usually built for mines, but this is the first in Cornwall, here used by a quarry.

King Arthur draws Excalibur from the stone. One of 73 stained glass windows created by Veronica Whall for King Arthur's Hall, a house in Fore Street Tintagel opened in 1933.

Trebarwith Strand once the centre of extensive slate quarries, with Dennis Head enclosing little Port William.

43

Trebarwith is an impressive sight in a gale, especially when the tide is high. Slate was loaded here too, though it was difficult, in days of sail, edging round Gull Rock, and not without casualties. Two of these included a sloop from Boscastle, the *Jane* in 1844, and the *Resolution* of Padstow in 1888. A sorry business altogether to raise a smile, but one vessel, from Clovelly engaged on the slate trade and wrecked locally was called *The Narrow Escape*. Adjacent Port William also had its hey-day as a port.

After a surprisingly wild and deserted stretch of coast the next little settlement is Port Gaverne. This was one of the busiest of the local slate ports so it makes a good place to

*Quarried slate from
Delabole being
loaded on to horse
drawn wagons to be
taken to Port
Gaverne.*

44

digress on the slate industry. Slate had a long history around this part of Cornwall; some of the early records being from 1396 in the reign of Richard II. However, it was the Industrial Revolution, with its concomitant demand for houses in the manufacturing towns that gave rise to the boom period in the nineteenth century. Delabole was the main centre, much of its slate having a characteristic reddish brown tinge. At the peak, in mid nineteenth century, over a thousand men were working in local quarries. The slate after being quarried, split and shaped had to be taken to the coast for shipping. Port Gaverne was one of the most important of these ports; there are records of a hundred horses on the beach at one time. However, as we have already seen it was only one port of many. Because of its brittle nature slate had to be handled with care, it was passed hand to hand and packed with hay in the ships' holds. The demand for slate was not only domestic; it was exported to the Continent and even the New World. It was the arrival of the North Cornwall Railway in the early 1890s that precipitated the decline in shipping.

Port Isaac is not far away and has a Canadian Terrace, so called by a returned emigrant, who struck it rich in Canada, and built the terrace on his return. It used to be a busy fishing

As location for TV's Doc Martin series Port Isaac attracts thousands of visitors. The beach is used as a car park but the incoming tide usually deters those who intend to dally!

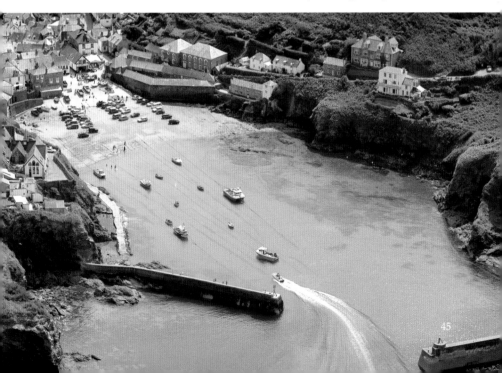

St Enodoc Church is not on the Coast Path but some walkers divert to see it. The church was once completely engulfed by sand, but was dug out and restored by 1864. Sir John Betjeman is buried in the churchyard.

port but there is much less done there now, just enough to give it an authentic smell!

The old port is huddled around an inlet of the sea and consequently the streets and alleys are narrow and space is generally restricted; so restricted that the central car park is on the harbour beach. This, not surprisingly being subject to the tides, does at least mean that they are not much burdened by over-lengthy parking! Port Isaac features as Port Wenn in a television comedy drama *Doc Martin*.

The path from Pine Haven to Portquin gives some exercise and scenic views. You may like to ponder, though, why Cornwall County Council fought so hard and spent so much money trying not to have a coastal path here that they could have had for free! Happily a public enquiry in 1983 put a stop to their ridiculous opposition, though they still engaged in a rearguard action by erecting an enormous fence which was nicknamed 'Hadrian's Fence'.

Lundy Hole has a spectacular collapsed cave. Pentire Point on the north side of the Camel Estuary provides perhaps the finest all round view of anywhere on the Coast Path in Cornwall. Not only can you look along the coast in both directions but you also have the wide sweep of the

Camel Estuary in view. Just before the Point is a small plaque to Laurence Binyon who was inspired by the scene to write his famous poem *For the Fallen,* the fourth stanza of which is recited every year on Armistice Day.

> *They shall grow not old, as we that are left grow old.*
> *Age shall not weary them, nor the years condemn.*
> *At the going down of the sun and in the morning*
> *We will remember them.*

Padstow is reached by ferry from Rock; there are records of a ferry here for over six hundred years. Think too of the hazard to seaward caused by the notorious Doom Bar. Over the years some five hundred ships, including no less than three lifeboats have come to grief over that treacherous sand bar. The daymark on Stepper Point ahead was built in an effort to reduce this loss. Some folk today associate Padstow with restaurants and fish on a plate. It was once a more considerable fishing port with regular trains of fish going up to Waterloo. Despite the Doom Bar a lot of shipping came and went here. Among the most interesting of cargoes to leave were the stones for Eddystone Lighthouse. The saddest

Looking north along the west bank of the Camel estuary, Padstow dominant on the left. Well beyond is Gun Point and finally Stepper Point with its tall daymark. On the other side of the estuary, nearly opposite Gun Point, is the notorious Doom Bar the graveyard of so many ships.

cargoes were the emigrants, with the decline of Cornish mining and the depression, ships from Bristol called here on their way to the New World.

Trevone is remarkable for its Round Hole, another collapsed cave. Harlyn Bay has an ancient burial ground. It was in use for an enormous span of time from 1900BC to 300BC. Many of the skulls of those buried were fractured, and it is assumed this was done after death with the idea of releasing the soul. Sometimes a frog was buried, either as food for the afterlife or as a talisman? A little girl had two mice buried with her, possibly for the same reason, or could they have been pets? We can only conjecture. Perhaps the saddest burials are of the three who may have been sacrificed to dedicate the cemetery.

Looking north along the east bank of the River Camel estuary. The sandy beach is Daymer Bay, beyond it is Trebetherick and then Polzeath. The headland in the distance is Pentire Point, perhaps providing the best all round view on the coast in Cornwall.

Bedruthan Steps is one of the well-known beauty spots on the Cornish Coast so do not expect to enjoy it alone. However it is worth seeing, so do not plan to walk by in the dark! On Trenance Head, just before Mawgan Porth, is an inconspicuous ditch which was once a canal that was intended to link in a semi-circular route Mawgan Porth, via St Columb Major and Minor, with St Columb Porth further down the coast. Authorised in 1773, construction work went on from 1775 to 1779, but it was never completed.

At Watergate Bay you are fast approaching Newquay. Later you pass Flory's or Black Humphrey's Island. The alternative name derives from an old recluse who once lived there in a disused mine working. He may have had seclusion, but he hardly had comfort, it is a draughty spot! Trevelgue Head has a superbly defensive Iron Age promontory fort, with no less than seven ramparts and ditches; excavations have proved it was in use over a long period; Pevsner suggests it was occupied 'from the Iron Age to the Dark Ages'.

SUGGESTIONS FOR SHORT WALKS

New Polzeath – Pentire Point

Park if you can on the seafront at New Polzeath, there is another large pay and display car park just inland. From the seafront car park walk back around the corner of the road to a Coast Path sign that says 'New Polzeath' one way and 'Port Quin' etc. the other. Take neither but go along the track with dwellings on the right which has a little notice 'Pentireglaze Haven'. Soon, where track swings left, go forward on the bridleway through a series of farm gates. On reaching the road turn left to go down in a dip and up the other side, then left again, signed 'Pentire Farm and Lead Mine' car park. (As you go through a gate you look forward across the mouth of the Camel to Stepper Point with its daymark and beyond to Trevose Head with its lighthouse). Soon the car park is on your right, enter. In the park by the information board a path goes right over the old spoil heaps. Bear slightly right to cross a field area to reach the Coast Path by an old stone stile,

The old lifeboat station at Hawker's Cove near Stepper Point. The lifeboat moved to a new location in Mother Ivy's Bay near Trevose Head in 1967.

49

turn left. (Soon good views back along north coast to Tintagel Island and beyond). Passing behind The Rumps to get to Pentire Point. (Pause here, some consider it the best coastal viewpoint in Cornwall). Then follow Coast Path back to New Polzeath. Just over 4 miles (6.4 km).

Mawgan Porth – Bedruthan Steps

Park at Mawgan Porth car park 850 672 and cross the road to the entrance of the beach. The Coast Path is signposted Porthcothan via Bedruthan and goes along the beach for a short while passing the lifeguard's lookout hut. It then goes up steps, climbs for a while, and dips to a stream to climb again up on to Trenance Point. (As you ascend, just before passing a large bungalow, is a shallow dip that has a shed and a greenhouse. This, though it is hard to believe, was the canal that went to St Columb). Continue northward, following the Coast Path until you come to Bedruthan Steps, the chain of rocky islets. (You do not have to believe the legend of the giant and his stepping stones to admire them!). The nearest building is the National Trust, Carnewas, that usually offers refreshment for a long season from mid February to mid-November. Thus fortified, return the way you came. If the tide is out, when you get to the stream you can descend the steps and walk back along the beach. Just over 4 miles (6.4 km).

The collection of seaweed was once commonplace around the Cornish coast where it was dried and spread on fields to add to their fertility. Here a pair of horses wait patiently while the cart is loaded.

CHAPTER 4
NEWQUAY TO PENZANCE

The path continues south-westerly passing Perranporth as far as Hayle. Here direction keeps changing to circumvent the Penwith peninsula, taking in St Ives and Land's End to finish at Penzance. Throughout nearly the whole of this section there is evidence of past mining activity. Much of the Penwith coast is granite, providing dramatic castellated scenery.

Newquay has an interesting past but the modern bustling, surfing resort belies it. In reality it has a multi-stage history. It started life, as a fishing village with a number of variations of name, one of them was Towan Blistra. Incidentally one of the earliest documents about Cornish mining dates from 1554 and records the search for silver around Newquay. In the sixteenth century a quay was built which led to the name Newquay, in the nineteenth century it became a port. The port was later purchased by the Cornish industrialist family

Newquay Harbour. The original village was a fishing community, next it became a commercial port exporting principally china clay, but today leisure is paramount.

Treffry, of Par, and used for the export of china clay until after World War I.

Beyond the harbour and up on a headland is the well known whitewashed Huer's Hut. Here lookout men waited for the reddish tinge in the sea that indicated the arrival of a shoal of pilchards. Having located them, the lookouts alerted the villagers and directed the fishing boats to the fish. The Gannel was once a busy trading river and as many as twenty schooners have been recorded waiting for a tide. Ships were built here and Clemens shipyard was well known in the days of sail. A canal to service the clay pits was projected, but the scheme was never started.

Chapel Rock off Perranporth. Needless to say it once had a chapel! The town's name comes from the Celtic saint St Pirran, and his oratory, perhaps the oldest complete. Sadly at present it is not open to the public.

Perranporth as it looked at the end of Queen Victoria's reign.

Crantock derives its name from Saint Carantocus and likes to remember the time when it was more important than Newquay. Then Newquay folk would come to do their shopping in Crantock not the other way round. Crantock was once famous, or possibly notorious, for its lack of any inns, because in 1800 the Temperance Guild bought all three public houses and closed them.

As you draw nearer to Perranporth you pass close to the site of St Piran's Oratory. It dates from the sixth century and is believed to be the oldest place of Christian worship in England with its four walls standing. We may gaze in awe at an ancient cathedral, say Salisbury, with its graceful spire; yet here,

humble though it may have been, is a site of Christian worship literally twice as old. It was unearthed from the sand dunes in 1840, and a concrete shell was erected over the building in 1909 but this proved insufficient to protect it. Unfortunately to prevent further deterioration the remains had to be reburied in late 1980. Perranporth, the name derived from St Piran, is fortunate in that a charity had the foresight to secure a long open space in the middle of the town. This has been used for a bowling green, boating lake and gardens. A café in the town once advertised as a specialty 'lemon mouse', we wonder did they cater for colour conscious cats!

The name Cligga is derived from the Cornish word 'cegar' meaning a precipice. This is the first place where granite can be seen on the coast. It is only in small quantities, but if the sun is shining, there will be the characteristic sparkle beneath your feet. The old works on Cligga Head manufactured dynamite. Obviously it was a very necessary ancillary industry to mining and quarrying, but not one that could happily be placed too near to habitation, hence its isolation. The factory was last used by the Nobel Explosives Company and was closed about 1920. The name Nobel is now associated with Peace Prizes but the industrial company provided the wherewithal.

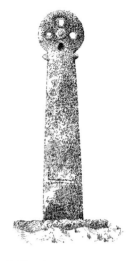

St Piran's cross, believed to be the oldest in Cornwall, stands not far from the ruins of St Piran's Chapel among the dunes at Penhale Sands.

The remnants of Cornwall's mining industry are to be found all round the coast. Closest to the sea is the Towan Roath Shaft of the Wheal Coates Mine near Chapel Porth. One of the best known and most photographed mine chimneys in Cornwall.

Trevaunce Cove. To the right of the picture there used to be a small harbour, taking in coal and sending out mineral ores. The builder was Henry Winstanley who built the first lighthouse on Eddystone. The harbour was badly damaged in a storm in 1915 and was never repaired.

At Hanover Cove look for the greenish tinge in the cliffs, evidence of copper ore. The name Hanover comes from a Falmouth packet boat of that name that was wrecked here in December 1763. Of more than 100 persons on board, only three were saved. Considerable efforts have been made at salvage, including a major one involving an oil rig, because the ship contained £60 000 in gold coin. No less than 54 cannon have been salvaged but not a great deal of bullion. It is an interesting thought that, while archaeology on land sites often only recovers what has been thrown away, archaeology under the sea can produce everything that was being used at a particular moment - like a time capsule.

Trevaunce Cove provided the port for the St Agnes area. The harbour was built by Henry Winstanley who also built the first Eddystone lighthouse and unfortunately he perished there. The harbour was destroyed after a breakthrough by the sea in 1915, but if the tide is right you can still see some remaining dressed blocks of stone lying on the beach. After Tubby's Head you pass close to the Towan Roath shaft of the Wheal Coates Mine, well known because of its use as the frontispiece to Daphne du Maurier's book *Vanishing Cornwall*. A mine in Cornwall could have several shafts each of them individually named.

Porthtowan had the very rich copper mine, Wheal Towan. Its owner was reputed to be making a guinea a minute; somehow £1.05 does not seem equivalent!

Portreath is much changed and some of the transformation is comparatively recent. It was once known as Bassett's Cove after the powerful local

family that did so much to improve the port. It exported copper ore to South Wales and imported coal to fuel the mine engines. The harbour walls and massive inclined plane attest to past activity. In fact the import of coal for domestic purposes went on until well after World War II. Heaps of coal and showers of coal dust were commonplace where the maisonettes now stand

It is easy to forget that Cornwall, now known as a holiday county, was once at the forefront of the Industrial Revolution, and Hayle was one of the hubs. It has always been a working place based on its priceless asset on this coast of a safe harbour. Although originally it was just a port, it grew to be an industrial town as well. The two halves of the town were named 'Copperhouse' and 'Foundry'. Harvey's engineering works started at the end of the eighteenth century and steadily grew in importance over a long period, until it became the largest engineering works of its kind in the whole of South West England. Not surprisingly their main business was with mine machinery, and their speciality was pumps. Their products went not only to Cornwall but also to mines throughout the United Kingdom. They had a considerable export trade selling irrigation machinery to Egypt. They also achieved a 'coals to Newcastle' act of selling pumps to the Dutch who, in connection with their dykes and reclamation schemes, were considered the foremost experts in Europe. The decline in mining affected Harvey's business and they diversified into shipbuilding. They launched the largest ship ever built in Cornwall, the *S.S.Ramleh*.

In 1884 Florence Nightingale Graham was born in Hayle, although her parents must have had expectations to give her names such as those; the true birth names probably mean little to anyone. At

The entrance to Portreath Harbour.

The photograph on the previous page shows Trevaunce Cove, near St Agnes, in 1894. Pitted and scarred by copper mineworks this area typifies the kind of industrial landscape which was to be found over much of Cornwall in the nineteenth century. Here we see the same cove today, and while some vestiges of mining remain, trees and bracken have returned to soften the landscape.

Looking along the coast westwards from Godrevy towards Hayle with its miles of beaches. The lighthouse was built in 1859 because of the number of ship-wrecks thereabouts on the notorious Stones Reef.

Looking upstream at the mouth of the Hayle River estuary. To the right Hayle lagoon a mecca for bird-watchers, the large urban area is Hayle itself.

the end of a life spent building up a worldwide beauty business, and incidentally making a fortune of five million, she was much better known by her trade name 'Elizabeth Arden'. At nearby Grigg's Forge, Bob Fitzsimmons, the only European to have won three world-boxing titles was apprenticed as a blacksmith.

On a hill above Carbis Bay is the sharply pointed 50-feet-high Knill Monument. It was erected by John Knill, a Mayor of St Ives, with the intention of being buried there; but over difficulties with consecration he was not. He is remembered

today, not only for the monument but because he left a bequest for a ceremony on St James Day, the 25 July, every fifth year. Ten girls dance around the monument to music played by a fiddler and two widows must attend. The ceremony takes place in the second and seventh year of each decade; therefore if you wish, you can time your walk to be there in time to see the next one!

St Ives was principally known as one of the great pilchard fishing towns of Cornwall, enormous quantities being landed here. The local museum has stencils once used in the export trade, such as Ancona, Bari, and Leghorn that show the extent of the trade. The harbour was improved by Smeaton who built the third Eddystone Lighthouse that has now been moved to Plymouth Hoe. There was also mining of both tin and copper here. The founder of the Salvation Army, the Rev. William Booth, led a mission to the town in 1861–62; there is a plaque commemorating this near the Lifeboat House. A colony of artists was founded here from the end of

A superb view over St Ives with the harbour in the foreground and the Island beyond. The startling blue/green of the sea and its reflected light is what first brought artists here in the late nineteenth century.

57

St Ives is fortunate to have two good beaches facing in different directions, this one is Porthmeor the other being Porthminster. The big white building just behind the beach is the Tate St Ives which draws thousands of visitors to the town which has a long tradition of working artists.

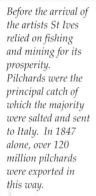

Before the arrival of the artists St Ives relied on fishing and mining for its prosperity. Pilchards were the principal catch of which the majority were salted and sent to Italy. In 1847 alone, over 120 million pilchards were exported in this way.

the nineteenth century. Nowadays St Ives is well known for its holiday trade, but the Great Western Railway's role in promoting it as the 'Naples of the West' is sometimes forgotten. Rosamund Pilcher the novelist was born in St Ives.

Porthzennor Cove, unlikely though it looks, once had a small fishing fleet operating from it. Zennor is well known for its mermaid on a church bench end. Many know the legend about it but few realize that she long predates the legend. Mermaids were a popular inclusion in Medieval Bestiaries and were often copied by wood carvers. D. H. Lawrence and his German wife Freda came to the area in

1916 and fell under local suspicion that they were spies. Virginia Woolf also lived here. Zennor has a small but interesting folk museum; much has been collected in a small space, but it is well worth seeing. We have memories of a farm bed and breakfast where the cows and calves had been separated that day. The night was disturbed by the constant mooing, so much so, that the lady of the party said at breakfast she looked forward to her next steak!

Gurnard's Head is another Iron Age promontory fort; such sites must often have been pretty bleak places in which to live. The obvious conclusion is that defensibility must have been more important than comfort. Geevor, nearby, was one of the last of the old tin mines to close in 1986. When it was working the sea here was often tinged with red, caused by the tin ore waste. The site is now a heritage museum The nearby Levant mine had workings extending under the sea. It was the last great copper mine to operate in Cornwall; at peak it had employed 500 men. It continued extracting tin until 1919 when the main engine for raising and lowering miners failed and 31 men were killed. In the 1930s the sea broke through into the disused undersea workings. However, in the 1960s, the reserves of tin of the nearby Geevor mine were low and so it was decided to try and plug the hole in the seabed. This extremely difficult engineering feat was accomplished despite adverse weather, and extraction of tin continued under a 600-ton concrete plug. The

Gurnard's Head provided an ideal site for an extensive Iron Age cliff castle. Living there for long must have been bleak, but a preferable option if your life was at stake.

Cape Cornwall. Notice the mine chimney on the tip, a distinctive feature but never very useful having problems with draught. On the left of the promontory are the walls of the one time garden where fruits, such as peaches and grapes, were grown in large greenhouses. This place is unique, being England's only cape (technically a cape is where two oceans or currents meet).

much-photographed Crown's Mine at Botallack is remembered for a visit of the then Prince and Princess of Wales in 1865. The princess, it is recorded, wore a white flannel cloak and white straw hat, both trimmed in blue. This sounds exotic, as would befit a princess, and the trimming no doubt was, but tin miners at that period did wear white flannel and straw hats, so she was only wearing standard mining gear!

There were once extensive greenhouses on Cape Cornwall growing fruit. A mine chimney dominates the headland but when in use was never a great success because of draught problems. Beyond and above Cape Cornwall is Ballowal Barrow, an elaborate and unusual Bronze Age burial cairn. Out to sea are the rocky islets, the Brisons, sometimes called the Sisters. In medieval times they were sometimes used to let malefactors consider the error of their ways. In Victorian times they became popular for picnics and later the aim of powerful swimmers who could master the strong currents encountered.

The name Sennen stems originally from the dedication of the village church to Saint Senana. The quay at the Cove was built to enable the lifeboat to be launched in stormy weather. Perhaps the fairest thing to say about Land's End is that it has suffered because of its popularity with tourists and its commercialisation. The best thing about it is undoubtedly

Sennen Cove; the lifeboat station with its launching ramp bottom left. Just to the right can be seen the round capstan house.

The Longships Lighthouse.

the seascape. On a really clear day there is the sight of the Isles of Scilly about 25 miles away, and usually there are views of the lighthouses on Wolf Rock and the Longships. There are numerous offshore rocks with names ranging from the humdrum Kettle's Bottom to the more sinister Shark's Fin. Even in comparatively calm weather the sea off Land's End is in a state of turmoil but in stormy weather the sight is much more dramatic. The Longships Lighthouse, built in 1873, is 50 feet high on a rock 60 feet tall yet, in a gale it can look most insecure.

Tol-Pedn-Penwith means the holed headland of Penwith, and what a dramatic hole it is, a collapsed cavern with a considerable drop. However, you need to seek it out as so many pass close by without seeing it. Out to sea is the Runnel Stone, which was a regular graveyard for ships, with no less than 30 steamers being wrecked or badly damaged there between 1880 and 1923. In 1923 the biggest vessel ever to be holed there, the *City of Westminster,* struck the reef. The impact broke off the entire top of the rock, and consequently, although it was the end of the ship, it was also the end of the stone as a serious hazard. The top that used to be awash is now 20 feet below the surface and no serious wreck has occurred since. Porthgwarra has a cave-like tunnel through which boats could be hauled up off the shore. It was reput-

The spectacular Minack open air theatre is sited on the clifftop close to Porthcurno.

edly here that the last large seine net catch of pilchards took place in 1916. At Penberth there is an old outdoors capstan used for hauling up fishing boats. St Loy has the reputation of being one of the warmest places in the country; the feral fuchsias and luxuriant hydrangeas would seem to confirm this. Tater-du is a modern lighthouse, only being built after the wreck in 1965 of the Spanish vessel *Juan Ferrer*. She went ashore at Carn Boscawen and eleven men were drowned.

Lamorna was a quiet place once and is relatively quiet again today, but in between it was for a while alive with the noise of quarrying. In Victorian times there was a great demand for granite in London and elsewhere for building and construction projects. Dartmoor had traditionally been a main source but it had to be taken to the coast before it could be shipped. This was labour intensive; here at Lamorna the granite was next to the sea. A pier was built in 1834–35 and the quarry continued in use until about 1910 with some of its output going to the Thames Embankment.

Mousehole is known these days either for its splendid display of Christmas lights, and from the childrens' story *The Mousehole Cat*. Once it was of more importance than Newlyn or even Penzance. It has its own chronicler in Nettie Pender who wrote of her early recollections there. Interesting reading it is too, highlighting as it does how much times have changed in living memory. Offshore is St Clement's

Land's End – walkers must be careful to turn left here! The prominent headland is correctly called Dr Syntax's Head. He was a fictional character of a certain William Combe. Of this writer it was said, however much he earned he could always spend more! Whatever else you may think about Land's End, the seascapes are superb, and if you are fortunate with conditions you will be able to see the Scilly Isles about 25 miles away.

Isle, where there was once a small chapel dedicated to that particular saint who was the patron saint of ships. The bird sanctuary, originally founded by the Yglesias sisters, was taken over by the RSPCA but is now an independent charity. They had a tremendous influx after the *Torrey Canon* disaster, treating over 8000 birds, but unfortunately few survived. Dylan Thomas spent his honeymoon here and, perhaps not unexpectedly, found the place lovely!

The rise of Newlyn was the cause of the decline of Mousehole. One of the factors in Newlyn's prosperity used to be the large Penlee Quarry that has now ceased working. This quarry had its own little railway line taking stone to the harbour at Newlyn. It was England's most westerly railway and therefore the unexpected answer to a favorite catch question among railway enthusiasts. For many years one of the engines was preserved on a concrete platform. Yellow and long funnelled, it looked exactly as if it came from the pages of a child's storybook. Newlyn is another place that has become famous for its artists. The Newlyn School, as it was called, started in the 1880s and amongst those who have lived and worked here was Dame Laura Knight, well known for her delightful studies of circus life. Passmore Edwards, a poor Cornish boy who worked hard and eventually grew up to riches, later becoming a philanthropist and was responsible for building Newlyn's Art Gallery.

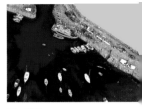

The lifeboat at Mousehole; the inhabitants like to remember times long ago when the place was more important than Newlyn or Penzance! Mousehole is known both for its display of lights at Christmas time and its sanctuary for injured birds.

Newlyn in the late 1890s looking along 'The Narrows' on the road towards Mousehole.

SUGGESTIONS FOR SHORT WALKS

The picture shows the typical rugged coastline of West Penwith. Despite the area being extensively mined, many of the ancient field patterns remain.

Godrevy and Navax Points

A short but scenic walk can be accomplished to Godrevy and Navax Points north of Gwithian. Park at the National Trust Godrevy car park 586 422 (there is another car park further on, but you did want a walk!). There is a café by the car park. Walk a few yards along the road and then go left to pick up the Coast Path unmarked at first but well worn. You can then walk out to Godrevy Point with its splendid views of Godrevy Island. From there continue to Navax Point going just beyond the old trig point now with the National Trust Navax Point sign to look north along the coast. Then return the way you came, surprising how different some of the views are. There is an obvious short cut back omitting Godrevy Head if you want to take it. (It is a particularly rewarding walk in spring when so many flowers are out.) Distance is just over 3½ miles (5.6 km).

St Ives – Lelant

A short walk that can be accomplished with the aid of a bus is Lelant to St Ives. It starts very easily but there are several climbs. Catch the bus at St Ives and get off in the main street of Lelant just before the Post Office. Walk back to the corner and take the road signposted Golf Course and St Uny Church. Go along this road to the church where the Coast Path leaves the road. Note the blocks of foundry slag used at the entrance to Lelant Church. Inside the church is a memorial to the Praed family who gave their name to Praed Street outside Paddington Station in London. The Coast Path goes down and under the railway line before turning left. Then follow the Coast Path all the way to St Ives. There are a few unmarked paths leading down to beaches but the Coast Path is usually clear. (Approaching St Ives you will see the Baulking House, a huer's lookout). If you want to get back to the bus starting point, turn left up the steps opposite the Pedn Olva Hotel. Refreshment at Carbis Bay and St Ives. Distance about 3½ miles (5.6 km).

CHAPTER 5
PENZANCE TO FALMOUTH

The route is at first south-east to Porthleven then south along the west coast of the Lizard peninsula. At the southerly point, direction alters to north-east to just beyond Coverack and then approximately north to Helford and north-east again to Falmouth. The Lizard provides, in a relatively small area, a great variety of scenery.

Surprisingly Penzance seems to hide its light under a bushel. It has so much of interest for visitors but somehow does not seem to make the most of what it has got. As you enter Penzance the war memorial is a good place to look back at the coast. Here the harbour area starts; the *Scillonian* the Isles of Scilly supply boat sails from here. It has to have a shallow draught to cope with its island route so many passengers find it upsetting! On the left there used to be a Trinity House depot which later became Trinity House National Lighthouse Centre, a museum, that too has closed. Outside the museum, and surprising many by their size, there were some huge sea-marking buoys. A large part of the old harbour has been turned into an extensive car park. Penzance Railway station opened in 1852 and it was the railway terminus that brought prosperity to the town. Before

Penzance is an access point for the Scilly Islands, being both the ferry port for the Scillonian and having the nearby Skybus airport at Land's End. It is also the terminus of the main railway line from Paddington. Note in the picture the prominent Lido swimming pool on the seafront.

the railway came the usual route to London was coach to Hayle, ship to Bristol, and then train to London. Think of the difference a direct train journey made. Regrettably the heliport that once offered a more rapid alternative route from Penzance to the Scilly Isles no longer operates.

The parish church of St Mary's was built in the 1830s and inside is a memorial to three fishing vessels that, on separate occasions, were each lost with all hands. There are several interesting buildings in Chapel Street. No. 25, a pleasant redbrick Georgian house, was once the home of Maria Branwell, the mother of the Bronte sisters. The Union Hotel, formerly a coaching inn, had an attached Georgian theatre, most likely designed by the same person as the famous theatre still surviving and restored in Richmond, Yorkshire. The most striking building though is the Egyptian House probably designed by John Foulston, the architect who planned the whole centre of Devonport. Market Jew Street has remarkable raised pavements the top of the street being dominated by the one time Market House that became a Lloyd's Bank, perhaps the most impressive commercial building in Penzance. Below the Market House is a statue of Humphrey Davy, inventor of the miner's safety lamp, who was a pupil at Penzance Grammar School.

Ladies on Penzance promenade c.1910.

The walk to Marazion is dominated by the offshore islet of St Michael's Mount. It was the site of a Celtic monastery that later became a Benedictine foundation until this was suppressed in 1425 when it became a nunnery until the Dissolution. After this it was given to Humphrey Arundell who joined the Prayer Book Rebellion. As a result, he not only lost his house; but also his head!

In the Civil War the Mount was held for the King but surrendered when the Royalist cause became hopeless. It now belongs to the National Trust. One of the things that surprises some visitors is that there used to be a herd of Jersey cows on the island. along with a purpose-built dairy.

The origin of the name Marazion and its alternative title Market Jew have been the subject of debate. It now seems agreed that the two names originally related to two different settlements that later grew together and coalesced. The meaning of the name Marazion was 'little market' and Market Jew 'Thursday market'. Marazion used to provide accommodation for the pilgrims who came to visit the Mount when it was a monastery. In medieval times it was probably one of the small Cornish towns that were represented by Members of Parliament, but later asked to be relieved of the burden because of the cost. Certainly it again had representation at the time of the Commonwealth.

The battleship HMS *Warspite*, that had served in both World Wars, ran aground at Prussia Cove in 1947 on her way to the breaker's yard.

St Michael's Mount lies off Marazion, a few miles east of Penzance. It is only an island at high tide, there being a causeway you can walk along when the tide is low. The Mount originally supported religious foundations, being first a Celtic and then a Benedictine monastery, and finally, up to the Dissolution, a nunnery. It became privately owned and was a Royalist fortress during the Civil War. It now belongs to the National Trust.

Bessy's Cove is called after a certain Bessy Burrows or Busslow who kept a local 'kiddley wink', a low alehouse. At one time it was relatively cheap to obtain a license to sell beer, but expensive for spirits. Therefore many opted for the cheaper license but sold spirits that would be produced if the customer winked when ordering. Shortly after Praa Sands, the path crosses Rinsey Head, with Wheal Prosper engine house. This mine produced both tin and copper ore. The engine house is now in the care of the National Trust and had been used in episodes of the television film *Poldark*. It was inland from here that in 1746 William Cookworthy, the Kingsbridge apothecary, discovered china clay in England. This discovery led to today's big extraction industry and incidentally to the 'Cornish Alps', clay waste tips, that are seen later from the Coast Path.

Hoe Point with Praa Sands often spelt Prah, though not everyone agrees with the OS. The village of Germoe lies behind. Out of the picture a little further east is Rinsey Head with its Wheal Prosper mine. It was inland from there that William Cookworthy discovered china clay.

Historically all parishioners had to be buried at their own parish church and nowhere else, presumably a safeguard against skullduggery? This ruling, whilst admirable inland, had an unfortunate consequence when drowned men were washed ashore. Because they were often not from that particular parish they could not be buried in church burial grounds there. This led to burials all along the coast where

wrecks occurred. The cross on Tregear Point just west of Porthleven is in memory of some of them. A local solicitor from Porthleven was responsible for the Grylls Act in 1808 that permitted the proper burial of those drowned, in consecrated ground.

Porthleven itself was of little significance in earlier times only becoming a harbour for fishing craft and a port in the nineteenth century. Unusually it faces the prevailing weather from the south-west so that the seas crashing against the harbour walls make a dramatic sight in storms. A local Methodist church is said to have inspired the following rhyme:

Porthleven has old records of a small fishing community but the harbour is not a port with a long history as it only dates from the nineteenth century. Its outer harbour wall that faces the prevailing weather is often photographed in gales. The town is remembered as boyhood home of Guy Gibson the Dam Busters VC.

> *They built the church, upon my word,*
> *As fine as any abbey;*
> *And they thought to cheat the Lord,*
> *And built the back part shabby.*

Guy Gibson, the Dam Busters VC, spent much of his boyhood in Porthleven and there is a street named after him. From Porthleven the Coast Path goes southwards across Loe

Today's walkers on the South West Coast path would hardly recognise Porthleven from this photograph taken c.1900 as houses now occupy the fields along the Loe Bar road.

Bar and passes the Anson Memorial. It comes first to Gunwalloe Fishing Cove, not much of a cove, and then to Gunwalloe Church Cove with its interesting old church. Reputedly treasure can be found on the beach here so it might be worth your while to abandon the Coast Path and walk across the beach!

Mullion Cove. The harbour here was completed in 1895 and is now owned by, but giving problems to, the National Trust. Offshore is Mullion Island known for its nesting seabirds.

Mullion Cove sometimes known a Porth Mellin, a pleasant spot but over-dominated by large hotel building on the cliff to the north. The little harbour was completed in 1895 but has more recently given concern to the National Trust who now own it. There used to be a lifeboat station here. Offshore is Mullion Island an important site for nesting seabirds. Gew-graze or Soapy Cove was an area where steatite, soapstone, was quarried. It was used for making porcelain, at Worcester for instance, and it was also used in

cosmetics and for fulling cloth. Kynance Cove is much visited, with good reason, so much so that special paths have been created to try and channel visitors' footsteps. Its name derives from the Cornish for ravine. Tony Collings called it 'a gem' but so rightly added 'in the rain, it can be as depressing as anywhere else'. At low tide it is possible to walk along the back of the beach, at high tide more energy will have to be expended!

The Lizard is the most southerly land in England and has an attraction all of its own and due to its geology and mild climate, a special flora. The true Lizard Point is about half a mile west of the road down to Polpeor and Polbream Coves where so many visitors trek. A direct line out to sea from the point would take you to Brazil. Pistol Meadows is another cliff-top burial ground for drowned seafarers. Lighthouses here have a long history, the first was a private enterprise affair built in 1619 by Sir John Killigrew. He erected it as an act of philanthropy, but hoped to levy a toll from passing ships to reimburse him for its maintenance. If you think about it, obviously, he would have difficulty collecting the toll, modest though it was! Furthermore the idea was unpopular with the natives who benefited from the shipwrecks! Trinity House took over in 1781 at first with oil lamps and then with electricity. At one time it was the most powerful lighthouse in the world. It was automated in 1998. In days of sail and before wireless, when communications

The Lizard lighthouse.

Kynance Cove, a place that has a long history of being on the tourist trail; so well visited in fact that special paths have been constructed. Nonetheless it is a place that should be seen. The name comes from the Cornish, meaning a ravine.

71

Near England's most southerly point, Pen Olver is the big headland, Bass Point beyond. Pen Olver has a place in radio history; Marconi used a hut here for some of his early experiments. The white building with battlements used to be a Lloyds Signal Station for shipping, but was later taken over by the Coastguard.

were much slower, ships from afar would often be directed to sail to 'The Lizard for orders'. In this way the owners could establish where the best price could be obtained at the time they arrived, for the cargo they were carrying, and then sail to London or Rotterdam or wherever. Unfortunately sometimes whilst waiting for their orders an unfavorable wind might take them ashore.

Shortly after the Lizard lighthouse is the Lion's Den, another spectacular collapsed cave. The new lifeboat station, opened in 1961, is at Kilcobben Cove, as it was considered that this was a less exposed situation than the old one at Polpeor Cove. Cadgwith is an attractive fishing village its cove divided by a little headland called the Todden. At Poltesco a now ruined water-powered serpentine works took over an old fishing station, the round building was a capstan house. Kennack Sands was described in 1948 as 'usually almost deserted'; one would hardly describe it thus in season today. Perhaps the kindest thing to say is that it is not typical of the Lizard. Soon the Coast Path takes you away to less developed countryside. Carrick-luz has a rare example of gabbro rock more commonly associated with Skye in the Inner Hebrides. Downas Cove is one of those tremendous down and ups that test a walker's stamina. Black Head in clear conditions is a great viewpoint, but after Chynalls Point another Iron Age fort, Coverack, is not far away.

Coverack is much used by walkers for refreshment or rest whilst traversing The Lizard. On arrival some turn early, missing the true Coast Path which goes out on to Dolor Point and then back past the Paris Hotel. This hotel is called not directly after the city but rather after a wrecked liner of that name. Coverack was the setting for a spectacular 'Songs of Praise' television broadcast some years ago. The path out to Lowland Point is on an area of raised beach, that is an area of coast that is now raised above sea level.

The path north from Lowland Point is a disappointing area of quarries and former quarries with the Coast Path often away from the sea. Offshore are the notorious Manacles Rocks that were reputed to have claimed a hundred ships and a thousand lives. Many of the victims are buried at St Keverne Church, where there is a cross erected to remember the *Mohegan*. She was wrecked in 1898, 49 were rescued but 107 lost their lives. At Porthallow the walker can regain his humour as the path returns to the coast. Porthallow marks the

Kynance lies on the south-west side of the Lizard and Cadgwith, seen here in 1894, is found just round the Lizard Point on the south-east. Today Cadgwith retains much of its old world charm.

73

Dinas Cove with Black Head and Coverack in the distance. Walkers will remember the steep ascent out of the cove, but the good news is that it is the last of that severity for some while. Black Head has a namesake farther down the cost.

halfway point from Minehead to the Path's end, and a marker is proposed. The Five Pilchards inn has many items of local interest.

From Porthallow the path goes northwards to Nare Point; not to be confused with the more dramatic Nare Head, also in Cornwall but over 25 path miles ahead. On your way from Porthallow you pass the scene of a shipwreck that occurred in the Great Blizzard of 1891. This was the large clipper the *Bay of Panama*, homeward bound from Calcutta with a cargo of jute for Dundee. Some of the crew saved themselves from drowning by climbing the rigging, only to be found frozen to death in the morning. Of a crew of 40 only 17 were saved. The path now turns eastwards to Gillan and Flushing, again there could be confusion here because there is another and bigger Flushing opposite Falmouth across the harbour. The hazard of Gillan

Looking across to Coverack c.1910. As today's walkers will find evident, quarrying was once an important industry along this part of the coast with the stone used in buildings locally and farther afield.

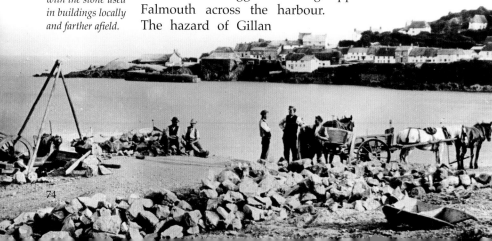

Creek has now to be overcome. At low tide one can wade across, whether the old seaweed-covered stepping stones help or are a further hazard is a matter of opinion. If the tide is high there is no alternative but to walk two sides of the creek through the little settlement of Carne. Those who take this route may spot on a wall an unusual flower container, a pottery saggar. In the days of coal-fired bottle kilns, pots were placed in these during firing. Folk with long memories might possibly remember the television program *What's Your Line* and one of the participants said he was a 'saggar maker's bottom knocker'.

St Anthony in Meneage – Meneage means 'monkish land' – has an unusual collection box which is a replica of the church itself. Behind is Dennis Head with its superb view points. It was an Iron Age camp and it was fortified by the Royalists in the Civil War, being one of the last fortresses to surrender. It is obvious what a strong position it would have been. Treath may well have once been the ferry point for crossing the river, but there is no point in waiting there now! The ferry to Helford Passage is now definitely in Helford. The river used to be busy with commerce going up to the port of Gweek. A little upstream from Helford is Frenchman's Creek well known thanks to Daphne du Maurier's book of that name. There are also oyster farms hereabouts.

This picture is interesting but requires explanation. The lower arm of the sea is the entrance to Gillan Creek. The top arm is the Helford River leading out into Falmouth Bay. The headland between the two arms of the sea is Dennis Head and the one above the top arm is Rosemullion Head. The close settlements at the bottom of the picture are Gillan on the right, Flushing (the Lizard one) on the left. Across Gillan Creek is St Anthony-in-Meneage.

Falmouth with Gyllyngvase Beach to the left of the picture. Looking across Falmouth can be seen the Inner Harbour and dock area. Penryn was the original port hereabouts Falmouth developed later and thrived in the days of the Falmouth Packets.

The ferry from Helford to Helford Passage is now purely for passengers, but cattle used to be taken. Durgan is an attractive spot where the former school, as elsewhere, is now a private house. Nearby are the famous Glendurgan Gardens; these were originally developed by the Fox family of Falmouth, Quaker shipowners and entrepreneurs. The property was given to the National Trust in 1982. Mawnan church is built on a prominent site overlooking the mouth of the Helford River. In fact there was a proposal in the nineteenth century by the coastguards to make it more visible by whitewashing the tower. Incredible as it may seem Rosemullion Head, a superb viewpoint, was originally omitted from the Coast Path. Beyond Maenporth (pronounced Mainporth) Beach the Aberdeen trawler *Ben Asdale* went

Helford Creek pictured around 1900.

ashore in a storm in 1978 resulting in a difficult helicopter rescue. On Pennance Point, a short distance before Falmouth, is a memorial to the men of the Home Guard who 'after the day's work nightly patrolled this coast armed and vigilant against German landings; thus they watched a thousand dawns appear across these great waters which form our country's moat'. Close by an old lead mine was converted in 1875 into an arsenic works. For about 15 years it was busy exporting arsenic, mostly to the USA, as a pest control for the cotton boll weevil.

The Home Guard memorial at Pennance Point.

Swanpool derives its name from its former use by the local Killigrew family for breeding swans. Pendennis Castle was one of Henry VIII's chain of south coast artillery castles. Its fine strategic position enabled it to withstand a long siege in the Civil War, being defended by the 80 year old Sir John Arundel. It was finally starved into surrender. Part of it is now a Youth Hostel.

SUGGESTIONS FOR SHORT WALKS

The Lizard

A walk around England's southern tip can be accomplished from Lizard Town where there is plenty of parking. Take the road east signposted Church Cove, presently there is a right fork signed Church Cove, take this past the church (worth a visit). At Church Cove turn right on the Coast Path. Proceed round Bass Point (Marconi Museum) passing old Lloyds signal station to Housel Bay. (Do not miss the Lion's Den collapsed cave just before the lighthouse. There is no sign but where the path takes a right-angled turn at end of a wall divert a few yards down to left by a notice saying Crumbling Cliff.) There is plenty of opportunity for refreshment where the road comes down to Polpeor Cove. Continue west passing Pistol Meadows (spare a thought for the drowned sailors buried here), to Old Lizard Head turning north. There are several paths and tracks back to Lizard Town but the one suggested is from Caerthillian Cove. As you go north you cross two small streams in succession, go up steps and there is a marker post pointing left for Coast Path right signed with blue arrow, take this. There are two signed footpaths right and unsigned ones left but continue with worn bridleway which becomes a lane to car park. The route is just over 4½ miles (7.2 km).

Falmouth Swanpool to Maenporth

A brief walk in the Falmouth area can be taken from Swanpool Beach. Park at the car park at the southern end of the lake, 801 313. Then walk up the road only a few yards to turn left on to the Coast Path. At first there is a rail fence on your right, a couple of yards after it ends there is a stile on your right. Go over this and proceed uphill alongside the hedge. There is a diagonal path across the field but this is not the one you want. At the top right corner of the field is the stone stile. (Look back at view). The path then crosses a golf course sometimes open sometimes enclosed. The last enclosed section has a well signed left turn and comes down to the Coast Path Turn right and continue along the Coast Path down to Maenporth. Here refreshment is usually available. Then return the way you came but this time stay on the Coast Path the whole way. In so doing you will pass the local Home Guard monument on Pennance Point. Later there is an unmarked stile on your right, do not take it but stay with the main path. Distance just over 3 miles (4.8 km).

Gyllyngvase Beach in 1903 with the collier Renwick run aground following a storm. Today's walkers follow the Coast Path along much the same route, although the scene inland is much changed.

CHAPTER 6
FALMOUTH TO LOOE

From Falmouth the first obstacle is crossing the mouth of one of Britain's finest natural harbours, the Carrick Roads (the name derives from a roadstead or safe anchorage, nearby, a 'carrick', a rock. In this case almost certainly Black Rock at the harbour mouth). Afterwards the coastline proceeds at first northwesterly and then westerly to Looe. Some have described this coast as Cornwall's softer shore, others have regarded the stretch from Place to Gorran Haven as the least visited by tourists.

Falmouth has much to offer and plenty of interest, including the unique claim to fame of having the only Marks & Spencer's you actually pass on the Coast Path! Perhaps surprisingly its growth to importance has been relatively recent; Penryn used to be the main town and port. Sir John Killigrew in the sixteenth century saw the potential of the fishing village of Falmouth, as it then was, and started to develop it. Later from the end of the seventeenth century for over 150 years to the mid-nineteenth century, Falmouth became a principal mail port with the sailings of the

Pendennis Castle on Pendennis Point at Falmouth, with the great natural harbour the Carrick Roads behind. Pendennis was one of Henry VIII's chain of artillery castles and endured a lengthy siege towards the end of the Civil War.

Looking across the Carrick Roads from Flushing (not the Lizard one) to Falmouth and beyond as far as The Lizard peninsula. The name Flushing is reputed to have been brought by Dutch settlers from Holland.

The Queen of the Fal getting up a good head of steam for her day tripper voyage upriver to Truro or St Mawes c.1900. Pendennis Castle can be seen on the Falmouth headland.

Falmouth Packets. There were for instance regular services to America, Brazil, Corfu, Gibraltar, Jamaica, Leeward Islands, Lisbon, Madeira, Malta, as well as other places. By 1795 a traveller wrote that Falmouth was the best trading and richest town in Cornwall. News of the victory of Trafalgar came ashore from HMS *Pickle* here in 1805 and was hastened to London. For many years Falmouth was the terminus for the London-to-Cornwall coaching service that was extended to Penzance in 1820. With the arrival of the Great Western Railway it also grew as a holiday resort. During World War II Falmouth became an important embarkation port for D-Day. More recently it has acquired an outpost of the National Maritime Museum.

On your way into the town you pass Arwennack Manor,

the one time home of the Killigrew family. It was used by Thomas Fairfax the Parliamentary Commander-in-Chief as his headquarters during the siege of Pendennis Castle. Ferries to St Mawes run all the year round except for winter Sundays. St Mawes has an attractive waterfront. It still retains an old Automobile Association (A.A.) town sign but this is an unusual one, it shows the last place on the road, Tregony, and of course the distance to London, but the next place along the road is not shown. Being at the end of the Roseland peninsula there was nowhere else to go, so the space for that name is left blank. It is easy to forget that in the

St Mawes left, the Roseland Peninsula right, with the Percuil River between. In the distance can be seen Gull Rock off Nare Head and beyond that again the Dodman. A hotel in St Mawes offered free winter holidays if it snowed whilst you were there. They never had to give one away!

Looking across the Roseland Peninsula to St Mawes, Towan Beach in the foreground.

early days of motoring the majority of road signs were not provided by government, either central or local. They were in fact the work of motoring and cycling organisations. One of the hotels in St Mawes used to run a promotion for winter holidays saying your holiday would be free if it snowed whilst you were there. They never had to give one away!

The ferry from St Mawes to Place is only seasonal. The walk round is about 9 miles but it does have its highlights. The first section, a walk along the shore of the Carrick Roads, is fine and the church at St Just-in-Roseland is considered by some to have the best setting in Cornwall. The last section the walk down besides the Percuil River from Froe is also fine. The large building at Place was once a manor

St Mawes Harbour in the early 1900s.

house of the Spray family, built on the site of the former priory. For a while after that it was an hotel. In front there are records of a tidal mill that was operational for three hundred years. Behind is the interesting church of St Anthony-in-Rose-land. Pevsner claims that it is 'the best example in the county of what a parish church looked like in the twelfth and thirteenth centuries... although much restored in 1850'.

The area of St Anthony's Head provides a series of wonderful viewpoints, the best of these looking across the water to Falmouth. Trinity House built the lighthouse in 1835. The fortifications, St Anthony's Battery above the lighthouse, were completed in 1885, but these have since been converted into National Trust letting accommodation..

Portscatho, the name means harbour of boats, was once a fishing village but is now a quiet resort. From Portscatho on, one walks along the shore of Gerrans Bay. In World War II the Royal Navy commissioned, as successors to the Loch Class frigates, a new Bay Class. They had such names as *Enard Bay*, on the Scottish West Coast, *Bigbury Bay*, in South Devon and *Gerrans Bay* here in Cornwall. However, with the end of the war this particular frigate was converted to a despatch vessel known as HMS *Surprise*. The climb to Nare Head is tough but the views are the reward; most walkers are keen to look out towards Gull Rock, but do not miss the vista southwards which enables you to see how far you have travelled, the Lizard already looks a long way behind. A German ship the *Hera* was wrecked on Gull Rock in 1914 and 19 men are

St Anthony's Head lighthouse from an early postcard.

Looking over Nare Head, Gerrans Bay beyond, towards Portscatho. In the distance, Kilberrick Cove, to the right. Nare Head affords another fine view but you will feel you have earned it after the double ascent to gain its top!

Caerhayes Castle.

Gorran Haven where tourism has displaced fishing as the main occupation in the town. The old coastguard row here is more impressive than it is in most places. The Haven takes its name from Gorran Church Town inland, an altogether smaller place.

buried in a mass grave at Veryan Church. Broom Parc shortly before Portloe, was used in the television production of Mary Wesley's *Camomile Lawn*. The location had initially been chosen from the air using a helicopter.

Portloe is an attractive village that has taken recycling to its heart; part of the *Lugger Hotel* was once a fish cellar and the church was a lifeboat house. The path proceeds in an undulating fashion through first West Portholland and then East Portholland. The double front doors against the sea are worth noting in the latter. Caerhayes Castle dominates Porthluney Cove. Hereabouts you are likely to be surprised by some long-haired, long-horned strangers from north of the border, Highland cattle. The first pair came as a gift, an unlikely sort of present some might think! The headland the Dodman is sadly a corruption of 'dead man' and must be related to the number of shipwrecks there. The views from Nare Head were good but from the Dodman they are even better.

Gorran Haven is another old fishing village that has turned to tourism. It has a street called Rattle Street because it was once cobbled and that was what the horse-drawn vehicles did! The old coastguard row is impressive. Offshore are the gruesome sounding Gwinges Rocks. On the way to Colona Point is Bodrugan's Leap. This is possibly a Cornish

Mevagissey, part in shadow part in sunlight, takes its name from two saints, Mevan and Issey. This seems at odds with its later reputation that its fishwives could make those at Billingsgate blush!

legend that has some factual basis. It is suggested that in the Wars of the Roses, Sir Henry Bodrugan was on the losing side at the time, and was pursued from his home by Sir Richard Edgecumbe. Sir Henry escaped to France by leaping over the cliffs to a waiting boat. Portmellon was engaged in shipbuilding until quite recently; a slipway remains.

Mevagissey's name originates from two saints St Mevan and St Issey. In the high days of the pilchard catch Mevagissey was well up in the league of Cornish fishing ports, and though it now still has a fleet it relies more on tourists. It has two harbours, the inner dating from the late eighteenth century, the outer was built about a hundred years later but

Mr Farrows, the coal merchant, stands on the quayside in Mevagissey surrounded by village children in 1913.

A Tea Treat railway excursion from St Austell to Pentewan c.1900.

The Square, at Pentewan c.1920

needed extensive renovation after the Great Blizzard of 1891. Pentewan, the emphasis as in so many three syllable Cornish names is on the second, first came to notice in medieval times for its stone, much used in local church building. Later it became a little china clay exporting port, with its own railway running down the valley from St Austell, opened in 1829. Coal was brought in as well as clay going out. The railway closed in 1918 but the harbour continued in use for another decade. In days when life was simpler and harder there are records of newly-married couples from St Austell going on the train for an evening honeymoon outing to Pentewan and back!

Black Head, do not confuse with the one south of Cover-ack, was another Iron Age coastal fort and later a rifle range. It was purchased by the National Trust and is a superb view-point. The wooded cliffs at Ropehaven are now a Cornwall Wildlife Trust nature reserve. The beach at Porthpean is often busy in season because St Austell is so near. Charlestown was once of no importance and called West Polmear. Then the Cornish entrepreneur Charles Rashleigh employed John Smeaton to build the harbour for the export of minerals and china clay from 1791 to 1800. It was afterwards called Charlestown after Rashleigh's first name and was used as a setting for the television serial *A Respectable Trade*. There is now a most interesting Shipwreck & Heritage Centre, well worth a visit. Par is another port kept busy exporting china clay. It was built by Joseph Treffry, a local land and mine owner, originally for the export of his mineral ores but later clay became the staple commodity.

Polkerris, although quiet now, was another busy fishing village for pilchards, in fact its cellar for processing them was among the biggest in Cornwall. There was a lifeboat station that was opened in 1859 but the boat was moved to Fowey in 1922. The lifeboat house was not wasted; it was turned into a beach shop. Trinity House erected the daymark on the

A spectacular view looking inland over Porthpean Beach towards St Austell and the distant china clay works, known as the 'Cornish Alps'. Walkers will find the stretch around St Austell bay relatively easy going between here and Fowey.

Daphne du Maurier

Looking across the Gribbin peninsula, towards Fowey and beyond. The red and white hoizontally-striped daymark is top right. The inlet middle picture, left of the daymark, is Polridmouth, that is usually pronounced without the 'ol'. This is close to Menabilly, Daphne du Maurier's one time home.

Gribbin in 1832; it is some 84 feet tall. Polridmouth is close to Daphne du Maurier's one time home at Menabilly. She used her own house as the basic idea for 'Manderley' in *Rebecca*. It was originally built by the Rashleigh family and is famous for its garden and grotto. The Coast Path at Polridmouth's easterly cove is unusual; here for a short distance it is a series of stepping-stones between a little lake and the shore.

Fowey, pronounced 'Foy', is approached by Castle Point with the ruin of Catherine's Castle, another of Henry VIII's artillery castles. The path drops down to the intriguingly-named Readymoney Cove; three different sources have offered three different origins for this name. The one that seems most plausible to me is 'ford by an ore/mineral house' but with place name origins plausibility is not necessarily the same as accuracy! Today, Fowey is a china clay port and holiday resort. One of the most exciting things you can see is a big empty clay boat coming upriver, dwarfing the water-front. The town has, however, a long and turbulent history. It was active as a port supporting the crusades and the Siege of Calais in 1347. Its seafarers, known as Fowey Gallants, harassed the French coast and in return the French came over and burnt the town in 1457. Later, when King Edward IV made peace with France in 1475, the men of Fowey were unwilling to desist harrying the French. The king had to use subterfuge and then send in rivals from Dartmouth to destroy their ships and remove the port's defensive chain. There was more conflict at Fowey during the Civil War. Essex

captured the town for Parliament but the Royalists recaptured it. Along with Daphne du Maurier, Fowey is associated with Arthur Quiller-Couch who used 'Q' as his pen name.

Across the water from Fowey is Polruan. It too had its own defensive castle to guard its own side of the river mouth. Once well known for shipbuilding and for pilchard fishing, it had a sardine canning factory before World War I. In the 1940s it had a rabbitry open to visitors but now there is not even a pastry crust to tell the tale (or should that be tail)!

Ascending the Coast Path you pass a grassy area owned by the National Trust. This was once a training area for the Royal Naval Reserve. Well into the beginning of the twentieth century, as many as three hundred men would come to Polruan for a month's training . At the top of the hill you can divert left into the car park, admittedly this sounds an odd suggestion for a walker. But Polruan claims, and not without reason, that it has the best view from any car park in Cornwall. Certainly it provides one of the best views of Fowey and Polruan.

There is a stiff climb before Pencarrow Head but the views are rewarding. The path passes the isolated Watch House,

Fowey from Polruan looking downriver, the view extending across the Gribbin peninsula. Pont Pill Creek can be seen bottom right (Pill, meaning creek or inlet). The quay at Polruan was once well known for pilchard fishing and shipbuilding, there was even a sardine cannery. Polruan had its own fortification too, known as the Blockhouse, a mini-fort, to parallel that of Fowey's, opposite.

Sir Arthur Quiller Couch became one of Cornwall's greatest literary figures. Publishing under the pen name Q, he was the author of many novels but is best remembered for his Oxford Book of English Verse. *Fowey was his home for many years.*

the only habitable building in some miles. Lansallos Church, inland, comes in sight and presently there is a rock-cut lane leading towards the sea. This route was deliberately cut out to enable carts to get down to the beach to bring up sand used to release nutrient in acid soils. After East Coombe there is a path leading inland to Little Lizard; this is where Marie Stopes, the birth control pioneer, had a house. There is an obelisk beside the path that is a daymark to warn shipping of the danger of the submerged Udder Rock out to sea. Its bell makes the right sort of mournful sound on a gloomy day.

Your first sight of Polperro is a large building, an old net loft, behind Peak Rock. It is difficult to be fair about this place; should one condemn it simply because it is so scenic and typical of a Cornish fishing village that at times visitors overrun it? It was once primarily a fishing port and is still one on a lesser scale today. Dr Jonathan Couch was born and lived most of his life here. He was a great naturalist and grandfather to Sir Arthur Quiller-Couch. Polperro is left by Reuben's Walk, named after a one-time harbourmaster.

You pass the remnants of early bulb fields on the way to Downend Point. Here is the wonderfully-sited town's war memorial, one thinks of others at Clovelly or Padstow, but this may be the best site of all. It will be no surprise in such a place to see that many of those commemorated were sailors. Unusually, of those named is a World War II member of the women's Auxiliary Territorial Service. The headland and the area around it was given to the National Trust by Angela Brazil, the author who wrote school stories for girls.

Proceeding along the shore of Talland Bay there is a large pair of landmarks. These are the western ones that measured a nautical mile for the Royal Navy's speed trials; you see the eastern ones later. You might also be intrigued to know that Talland Bay was the scene of Cornish smuggling brought up-to-date with the discovery of a more recent haul of drugs following which, arrests were made. Shortly there is an unnamed headland above Bridge Rocks. This is another compulsory viewing point unless the weather is foul. If it is clear out to sea Eddystone Lighthouse is visible; closer to hand is your best sighting of Looe Island. You can also see a part of Looe itself, and before it the eastern end of the Royal Navy's measured nautical mile landmarks.

Looe Island is also called St George's Island, and in the past was called St Michael's or even St Nicholas's Island. No one seems to know why there have been so many changes of name. There was a Celtic chapel on the island, rebuilt in medieval times. The island was bombed in World War II reportedly being mistaken for a British warship! It was owned by the Atkins sisters who wrote books about it. The best-known being *We bought an Island* by Evelyn E. Atkins. The island was gifted by the sisters to the Cornwall Naturalist Trust as a nature reserve.

Looe Island, also called St George's Island, it is now a nature reserve. It had a Celtic and then a medieval monastery.

SUGGESTIONS FOR SHORT WALKS

St Anthony's Head

A splendid walk around St Anthony's Head can be started from the National Trust car park at Porth Farm 867 329. The lower park is better because the path actually starts from there. The sign says Place, the path goes down to and then follows Porth Creek, and later down the Percuil River. There are several paths signed inland to Bohortha, ignore them all. You arrive at a road here, turn left though the unhelpful sign has its back to you. (There was tidal mill here for 300 years). You now follow the Coast Path signs, go up the road passing the entrance to Place House. Shortly turn right, but watch for the sign it is not well-positioned; go past the old church (the best example in Cornwall of what a church used to look like). The path for a while is sinuous but well way-marked except when you come down to a track there is no sign to tell you to turn left. Then simply follow the Coast Path all the way round St Anthony's Head (once fortified) and Zone Point. You pass N.T. signs for Porthbeor and Killigeran until you reach Towan Beach. Here you come down to a track with a blue arrow bridleway sign pointing left that also says Porth Farm car park. This is the way you want so leave the Coast

Path here. The distance is a little over 6 miles (9.6 km). An alternative start could be made from St Mawes by using the seasonal ferry to Place.

Fowey – Polruan

This walk is called the Hall Walk and admittedly uses very little of the Coast Path. Cross from Fowey on the floating bridge ferry to Bodinnick. There are several car parks close by on the Fowey side. On landing, go straight up the road passing The Ferry Inn on the left. A little further on, immediately after a small bend, you come to an entrance in the wall on the right with a notice 'Hall Walk'; turn in here. The first thing of interest is a Fowey war memorial (a good view across Fowey to St Catherine's Castle). Later, in a shelter, is a plaque telling how Charles I was nearly killed here. Almost immediately is the memorial to Sir Arthur Quiller-Couch. (The view is superb and has lengthened to the Daymark on the Gribbin and beyond to the Dodman). The path continues at high level for a while to come out into a field. It very soon turns right through a gate into a wood, no sign at the time of writing. The path then descends through a wood, but watch for a sharp right turn signposted Polruan to bring you out on Pont Pill Creek (a National Trust booklet describes it as a 'silent private place where old boats go to die'). Cross the bridge (note the limekiln on the right), take the path forward by the cottages, shortly turning right up steps into fields. Go through three fields, the first two climbing, the third nearly level. Cross the stile on a path then fork right and after a descent bear left keeping with the better used path. You come out on a minor road to turn right and very shortly leave the road to go left. Ignore two minor paths going right. The path becomes urban and concrete. When you reach a road turn right passing Studio Cottage to go down steep steps. Turn left to go along a road to the centre of Polruan and here turn right down to the quay and the passenger ferry back to Fowey. The distance given at the start of the Hall Walk is 4 miles; my measurement was a bit less however there is half a mile back through Fowey if you need to regain your car. Therefore say 4½ miles (7.2 km).

The memorial to Sir Arthur Quiller Couch.

CHAPTER 7
LOOE TO SALCOMBE

The route from Looe goes eastwards to Plymouth and then south-eastwards to reach Salcombe at the southern end of Devon's South Hams area. Plymouth is the biggest built up area on the Coast Path but nonetheless provides some interesting walking. Although they present crossing problems, the series of river mouths Tamar, Yealm, Erme, and Avon have a high scenic value.

Looe was for many centuries two distinct boroughs, West Looe and East Looe, both, believe it or not, sending two members to Parliament. Daniel Defoe on his travels visited the towns and wrote accordingly. 'Were they put together, they would make a very handsome seaport town. They have a great fishing trade here... but as to sending four members to the British Parliament, which is as many as the city of London chooses, that I confess seems a little scandalous.' The seven-arched bridge is the central feature of the place nowadays but bridging has a long history here. Work was started on a bridge to link the two boroughs of West and East Looe early in the fifteenth century. It was built, along with a chapel

Looking over West Looe to East Looe, they both once sent two Members to Parliament the same total as represented the City of London.

93

The seven-arched bridge is a central feature of Looe.

Local children fishing from West Looe Quay c.1920. The large houses on the riverside belonged to the wealthier members of West Looe society. A popular Looe saying is that East Looe is the sunny side and West Looe is the money side. The bridge can been seen in the distance.

to St Anne which stood in the middle of the bridge. By1687 the bridge was reported as being in decay and it had to be continually repaired. Finally, in 1853, the old one was pulled down and a new bridge was built 100 yards further upstream. Once mainly catching pilchards, the fishermen are now more ambitious in pursuing sharks!

Along the coast you come to Seaton. This has confused some because there is a bigger Seaton you go through later in Devon. It once had a sizeable holiday camp but, as elsewhere, a housing estate has now taken over the site. Shortly comes the somewhat larger Downderry where for a while you can walk on the seawall rather than the road. After the ascent of Batten Cliffs there are good views forward towards Rame Head. If you are of an introspective frame of mind you can ask yourself why it took thirty years to obtain a walking route here? Portwrinkle once had its little harbour; you can plainly see where it was and why it is no longer used. The Whitsand Bay Hotel is interesting in that it was originally built in Victorian times as a private house, at Torpoint, and only later moved to its present position. Most hotels let the guests come to them, not the other way around!

The route through Tregantle Fort, when the range is not in use, also took many years to negotiate. There was a grand opening day and the army provided the lunch. Older attendees with long memories of service food were amazed and delighted at the fare offered. Tregantle is one of the chain of forts built around the Plymouth area to protect the important Royal Naval Dockyard.

Seaton and its, beach. This is Seaton in Cornwall not to be confused with Seaton in East Devon. The rivers however are not so confusing; the rivermouth shown to the right of the picture is the River Seaton but the river at the Devon Seaton is the River Axe.

The walk along Whitsand Bay is not everyone's favourite although it has been improved from the time it was nearly all road walking. Polhawn Fort was built to guard against landings in Whitsand Bay, and it had a drawbridge that was raised each evening and lowered each morning. It was manned right up until 1926. Rame Head is another fine viewpoint and was once in the care of Tavistock Abbey. Shortly after Rame Head, but a little inland, is Rame Church, still lit by candlelight. After Penlee Point the path picks up the Earl's Drive, a carriageway made for Mount Edgcumbe, the stately mansion above the Cremyll Ferry. A row of buildings after Penlee was a Trinity House Fog Signal Station, the locals called it the 'Penlee 'ooter'. Cawsand Square has an

Cawsand to the left, Kingsand to the right. The former has always been in Cornwall but the latter was once in Devon. Fish cellars were built in Kingsand for the landing and processing of fish so the duties that were payable in Plymouth could be evaded.

almost Continental flavour. Kingsand follows, but do not miss the old county boundary sign between the two. Kingsand had fish cellars built by Plymouth merchants to avoid paying duties to the Duchy of Cornwall, which they had to do, if fish were landed in Plymouth. Picklecombe Point was once a fort but has been turned into residential accommodation. As you progress along the Earl's Drive again there is an unusual summerhouse; it is part of a recycled church from Stonehouse in Plymouth! Drake's Island is close by; originally having successive chapels, it later became a fortress. After the Civil War it was used as a prison for some Parliamentarians. Major-General Lambert was confined on the Island from 1670 until his death in 1684. A Danish ship was wrecked there in 1786 carrying a cargo of reindeer hides. Since 1973 these have been raised, the salt washed out, reprocessed and used as leather. Prince Charles had a pair of shoes made from them.

Up on the hillside is a ruin, a folly tower that was built at a time when it was thought very fashionable to have a ruin on your estate! Barn Pool looks quiet now but was very busy once, being used as an embarkation area before D-Day in World War II. The Edgcumbe family as they prospered, moved downriver to own the estate here, the original house being built in 1547. It was remodelled over the centuries only to suffer disaster, being destroyed by fire after bombing in 1941. It was rebuilt post-war. The Spanish Duke of Medina Sidonia was entertained here in 1554; he was so impressed, he thought he might make it his

An early nineteenth century print depicting the view from Mount Edgcumbe over the River Tamar and to Devonport Dockyard beyond. Designed by Victorian architect Sir John Rennie and constructed between 1825 and 1831, Royal William Yard is steeped in history and the Grade 1 former Royal Naval victualling buildings are coming alive with cafes, bars, restaurants and galleries.

English home after the Armada, of which he was the Spanish Commander-in-Chief. Needless to say he lost the away match so never had the opportunity! There is an obelisk in the park erected by one Countess Mount Edgcumbe in memory of her pet pig! Is that what is meant by aristocratic eccentricity? The Cremyll Ferry carries you across to Plymouth and Devon. The pay kiosk was once a tollhouse when there was a carriage road here. An inscription states rather sternly: 'Does thou love life? Then do not squander time'. The name Cremyll derives from the same source as the Kremlin in Moscow, variations of a Scandinavian word meaning fortress or strong place.

Originally Plymouth was to be another omission in the Countryside Commission's strange idea of a non-continuous path. However, since those days, sense has been applied and you can now walk the whole way through. Plymouth too has launched their own Waterfront Walkway, a project which has shown good results despite the fact that more needs to be done. One of the imaginative things that Plymouth has done is to highlight and often 'illustrate' places and things of interest along the way. Because Plymouth has such a varied and interesting history a whole book could be written about it – in fact several have. This volume will confine itself to one paragraph of general history and then just mention a few items of interest close to the route.

Plymouth's early development was stultified by a major portion belonging to Plympton Priory. This meant that in early medieval days places such as Dartmouth were more important ports. However by the end of the Middle Ages Plymouth was locally in the ascendant and it flourished in the Elizabethan era. A new naval dockyard was built at Dock, later Devonport, towards the end of the seventeenth century. The modern Plymouth is an amalgam of the three towns of Plymouth, Stonehouse and Devonport. Undoubtedly it has been wars, principally with Spain, France and Germany that have propelled the town's growth. War, however, exacted a terrible price in World War II, the centre of the city was destroyed and about 1000 people were killed by air raids.

King William Victualling Yard is in fact better seen from the Cremyll Ferry than it is at present from the route of the

A lighthouse on the Breakwater at the entrance to Plymouth Sound. The Breakwater took 30 years to build; it could be said to be the equivalent in engineering terms of the Channel Tunnel of its day. It was built to protect Plymouth Sound from the prevailing south-westerly weather. Until it was built the fleet had to use Torbay as an alternative supply base when the weather was unfavourable at Plymouth.

Plymouth Hoe perhaps provides the best urban view in Britain. Behind lies the city of Plymouth and beyond the distant hills of Dartmoor. Striped Smeaton's Tower, formerly the Eddystone's third lighthouse, is clearly visible. The swimming pool below is Tinside, recently refurbished and reopened.

path. However, this should alter as the one time supply depot is currently being converted into a housing complex and we are promised a path seaward of it. Pevsner claims it is 'by far the most impressive single architectural group in Plymouth'. In its working life it included a bakery, brewery, cooperage, mill, slaughterhouse, storage areas and of course offices. Devil's Point is where naval wives and families came to wave goodbye to their serving husbands and fathers. In pre-war days the usual commission, time away from base, was two and a half years! In Durnford Street are the Royal Marine Barracks. Millbay Docks was once busy with incoming liners that were met by boat trains. A plaque records some of the famous folk who were aboard including Cary Grant, Noel Coward, Lloyd George, Rex Harrison, Cecil Rhodes and H.G. Wells There is still commercial traffic today,

as well as ferry crossings to Roscoff in France and Santander in Spain.

The route circumvents the West Hoe and then comes to the Hoe itself; passing the place where Francis Chichester came to land in 1967 after his solo navigation of the globe. On the seaward side is the Tinside Lido, first opened in 1935, later allowed to decline but now restored. On the landward side is the Hoe itself. It has been described as the best urban viewpoint in England. It has of course the famous statue of Sir Francis Drake who also completed a circumnavigation of the globe. Smeaton's Tower, that was the third lighthouse to be built on the Eddystone Rocks in 1759, was transported here after its foundations became insecure. This is the same John Smeaton who we have already mentioned at St Ives and Charlestown. The tower's stump on the Eddystone rocks sits

In the cloud's shadow on the left is Plymouth Citadel, a dramatic 17th century fortress built to defend the coastline from the Dutch. Today it is home to the Royal Marines. Behind this is Queen Anne's Battery with yachts and pleasure craft lining the marina. To the far right is the National Marine Aquarium.

T.E. Lawrence in his working overalls on Flagstaff Quay c.1930.

An historic picture taken from RAF Mount Batten, c.1941. Beyond the Sunderland flying boat is the giant battleship HMS Hood steaming out of Plymouth Sound from Devonport. Two months after this picture was taken HMS Hood was blown up and sunk with the loss of most of the ship's company.

beside the present lighthouse that was erected by James Douglass in 1882, automated a hundred years later.

Proceeding from the Hoe the Citadel is up on the left, and the way is down to the historic Barbican. The most famous sailing from here was the *Mayflower*, a voyage that has brought Plymouth prestige and considerable tourist traffic, much it should be said to Dartmouth's chagrin because the *Mayflower* had originally sailed from there and it was only leaks in her sister ship the *Speedwell* that caused her to call at Plymouth! The way is now across the dock-gates of Sutton Harbour. The splendid new Aquarium is on the left – if you have time for fish! The route is now near the Cattewater, across the Laira Bridge to Orestone. Alexander Selkirk, the supposed inspiration for the fictional *Robinson Crusoe* lived here. Radford Lake is close by the site of the mansion, demolished in 1937, where Sir Walter Raleigh came on his return from the failed Guiana expedition in 1618. Turnchapel is quiet now although it is not so long since there were regular ferry services to Plymouth, and it was also the terminus of a railway line.

Mount Batten is a late but welcome addition to the Coast Path. It was an Iron Age site, and hard fought over in the Civil War. The hotel was once surprisingly a guano processing plant! For a while, including during World War II, it was a seaplane base and it used to be a great spectacle to see the Sunderland Flying-boats take off out to sea. Aircraftsman Shaw, Lawrence of Arabia, served here. Off Jennycliff, up until 1924, there were moorings for hospital ships with suspected plague and cholera victims. The high-level path on Staddon Heights gives a good view of the Breakwater. This was the Channel Tunnel of its day, taking 30 years to build. It was started in 1812 and at peak 700 men were employed on the enterprise. Until the lighthouses were built

Wembury. St Werburgh's Church, near the bottom of the picture, has associations with the founding of Western Australia. Back right is the mouth of the River Yealm pronounced 'Yam'.

it had a refuge for shipwrecked mariners. The Breakwater Fort was well thought out. It is close but has no contact with the Breakwater, so could not be rushed by men landing there. The Breakwater was built because the Sound was not a safe anchorage in the prevailing south-westerly heavy weather. For many years Torbay had been used as an alternative supply base when conditions were unfavourable at Plymouth.

Fort Bovisand was a fresh-watering point for the fleet, saving the longer sail up to Devonport. There is an unusual footbridge built over an inclined plane. Wembury looks out on to yet another Mew Stone, and is interesting for several reasons. John Galsworthy used it as his setting for Soames Forsyte's return to find his ancestors in *Swan Song*. The church dedicated to St Werburgh is on a commanding position above the sea and holds evidence of a connection with Western Australia. A local family, the Lockyers, provided the commander, a Major Edmund Lockyer, of the first expedition to settle in Western Australia in 1826, at Albany in the far south. There is a replica of his ship the brig *Amity* at Albany. When you read of the numbers on board, as well as the animals, you realise it must have been more than crowded!

John Galsworthy

On the Yealm is Noss Mayo, but the church here only dates back to 1882 with the original church now a partial ruin being some distance on by Stoke Beach. Several miles of pleasant easy walking is now on Lady Baring's carriage drive. It passes Warren Cottage where the warrener who

Near the mouth of the River Yealm, the Coast Path shows up clearly on Warren Point, the peninsula on the left descending to the ferry point. The village towards the back of the picture is Newton Ferrers.

Meadowfoot Beach, just right of centre. Further to the right is the mouth of the River Erme.

would then have farmed rabbits resided. The old church of St Peter once had no rights of burial and dead parishioners had to be taken to the mother church of Yealmpton some miles away. A petition was raised saying not only was the way sometimes treacherous but whilst the burial party was away the King's enemies might sail in and burn and despoil the area! Their petition was granted. After Stoke Beach on Beacon Hill there is a ruined tower that became a teahouse. When parties set out to be driven round the carriage drive in an anticlockwise direction, servants were sent out the shorter distance clockwise to prepare tea for the guests at the tower. The drive was made using unemployed fishermen and there is a story told, possibly apocryphal, about it. On the day it was finished his lordship came out and found a disconsolate workman sitting beside the finished drive. He enquired why the man was sad. 'Because sir there is no more work' was the reply. 'That is alright' said his lordship 'start again and make it wider!'

St Anchorite's Rock has been so called for many years; though there are no records of a hermit ever having been there. Behind Meadowfoot Beach with its bathing house is Mothecombe House which Pevsner claims 'makes a delightful picture'. Of more interest to some walkers, in a stretch of coast with few opportunities for refreshment, is a seasonal café in the old schoolhouse close by. The Erme can be waded

Looking down-stream towards the mouth of the River Erme, often regarded as the least spoilt river mouth in England.

at low tide along the line of the old ford. Behind Wonwell Beach (pronounced without the second 'w') is the much overgrown ruin of the pilot's cottage from the days when small ships still went upriver for Modbury. Bigbury-on-Sea has Burgh Island lying offshore. In truth it is only an island at high tide but there is a special sea-tractor which can still take you across dry-shod. The island originally had a medieval chapel dedicated to St Michael and now has an old inn and an Art Deco hotel. Guests at the latter have included Agatha Christie, Edward, Prince of Wales, later briefly King Edward VIII, and a certain Wallis Simpson. The island is supposed to have inspired two of Agatha Christie's works *Evil Under The*

The view west-wards from Burgh Island; a true island at high tide. To the right Bigbury-on-Sea and just beyond it Challaborough.

The Thurlestone.

Sun, and what is now known in these days of political correctness as *And Then There Were None*. Bantham, now known mostly as a pleasure and surfing beach, had an ancient past. There were settlements here at least from the fifth to the seventh century and it seems likely from the finds that it was a port engaged in trade. This theory is backed because undersea work off the mouth of the Avon has located a vessel carrying Byzantine pottery, and another with ingots of tin.

Thurlestone takes its name from the 'thirled' or holed stone, a natural arch mentioned in a Saxon charter, but happily still there to this day. The big local hotel was for a while in World War II an officer's training establishment. Service protocol ruled that you were only told the result of your course, passed or failed, at your home base. So officially you left not knowing. However, if you had passed you were already an officer so a taxi took you to the station at Kingsbridge. If a lorry came for you –you knew the worst – you had failed! The Belgian ship the *Louis Schid* was wrecked offshore in December 1939.

Nowadays most people call all this Hope Cove, the traditional Outer Hope to the left, Inner to the right.

Traditionally there were two Hopes, Outer and Inner, and some rivalry between them. Nowadays most refer to both as Hope Cove and leave it at that. There is an old row of former Coastguard cottages and an old Lifeboat Station. The lifeboat here was propelled by sails and oars but became a powered

boat when moved to South Sands at Salcombe in 1887. Later still the lifeboat was transferred to Salcombe itself.

The stretch of walking from Hope to Salcombe is first class, including both Bolt Tail and Bolt Head. Bolt Tail is an Iron Age promontory fort and on a clear day gives good views not only down to Rame Head but further beyond into Cornwall. Inland there are views of south-west Dartmoor. Ramillies Cove is a reminder of a terrible shipwreck here of the warship *Ramillies* in 1760. From a crew of 734 only 26 were saved.

On Bolberry Down was one of the first Radar Stations of World War II. It was, as they said in those days, extremely 'hush hush'. The Port Light Hotel was once a golf club house, but do not hasten for a club as the course closed in 1909. The radio mast is a Decca navigation station. The rocky islet, the Ham Stone, is off Soar Mill Cove and this is where the clipper ship *Herzogin Cecilie* came to grief in 1936. Bolt Head had another World War II lookout. After Starehole Bay you pick up the rocky but splendid Courtenay Walk, so called after the Courtenay family from Powderham on the Exe who owned sizeable estates in the South Hams. The route passes below 'Overbecks' now a National Trust property; it has sub-tropical gardens and an interesting museum. From North Sands can be seen the squat ruined tower of Fort Charles, or Salcombe Castle. It was another of Henry VIII's artillery castles and was the last Royalist stronghold in Devon to surrender at the end of the Civil War.

Herzogin Cecilie *was a German four-mast barque, built in 1902. She left Australia on 21 January 1935, with a cargo of wheat, and reached Falmouth on 18 May making her passage of 86 days the second fastest ever.* Herzogin Cecilie *was making for Ipswich in dense fog, when, on 25 April 1936, she grounded on Ham Stone Rock and drifted on to the cliffs off Soar Mill Cove.*

SUGGESTIONS FOR SHORT WALKS

Noss Mayo

Park at Noss Mayo car park next to the tennis courts at 546 473. This walk is a circuit but by going the way we suggest you get over the worst hill and least scenic section at the start.

The South West Coast Path originated as a route for the Coastguard to walk from lighthouse to lighthouse patrolling for smugglers. Today significant sections of the path are maintained and waymarked by the National Trust, which owns parts of the coast.

Exit the car park turning left up the road that deteriorates into a stony lane. At the top of the hill you join a metalled road turn left but very shortly right along a footpath, signed 'link to Coast Path'. There is a National Trust car park next to the footpath. The footpath leads down to a stile, go over it to follow the track bearing right. In a short while you join Lady Baring's carriage drive, that is the Coast Path, keeping right. Then simply follow the well graded easy walking of the carriage drive it is waymarked with acorns, ignoring all side paths. You pass Warren Cottage and later the path turns significantly right at the mouth of the Yealm. (Behind the second length of wall is a seat with a wonderful view). The path goes through a wood, passing a housing terrace on the right which was the one time Coastguard Row. You pass a large building with a small spire, the last part is called Battery Cottage, the name is on the house wall but you have to look for it. The path starts to descend and shortly by an information board 'Passage Wood' the path leaves the carriage drive going down steps left. This path dips to the old ferry point, with its tariff board on the right; look for this. The path, now a track, rises slightly to rejoin the drive just after a letter box in a brick pillar. Go ahead for a few yards and at a small parking bay there is a footpath slightly to the right going up a slope, take this. There is a National Trust sign saying 'Ferry Wood'. Walk through the woods and at the end you come down the steps to join the drive where you go right. (You can cheat by walking back along the road but check your insurance, there is more traffic than you might imagine). Continue along the road through Noss Mayo; ignore all turnings off to proceed up a slope. At the top bear right to car park.

Distance is about 4 ½ miles (7.2 km).

Bolt Head - Salcombe

Park at 'Overbecks' National Trust property at Salcombe. 730 373.

The crafty idea here is to park in the wide driveway at the bottom, this way you avoid a steep hill at the end of the walk. However space is limited and you may have to drive further up. Walk up the hill passing the entrance to the house; the path winds a little then swings right. Just as the slope eases there are steps going up left, take these. There follows a splendid high level walk to a direction indicator at Sharp Tor. Stop at this good viewpoint. The path goes right and starts to descend, ignore path going right, signposted Soar Mill Cove 3 m, continue down hill. Cross a stream by a stone bridge and come out into a field. Go up a short distance diagonally to the right to come to a pedestrian gate, follow a distinct grass path through two fields. In the second field there is some rough ground then a prominent white rock, keep right of it. Pass through another gate then turn left, signposted Bolt Head ½ mile, down the slope to pick up the Coast path to go around Bolt Head. The only place you might go wrong is where two footpaths meet just before the Head. Here the more scenic route is bearing right down a wide gully sign-posted Salcombe 2¾, not the path signposted Salcombe 2½ m. Descend the gully, fork left at Bolt Head and shortly stop again at the stone seat for another wonderful view. Drop down to Starehole Bay, ignore the path going left inland and follow the Coast Path back to 'Overbecks' car park. The distance is less than 4 miles (6.4 km.) but it is not a walk to be hurried.

South Sands at Salcombe. The resort is fortunate in having several beaches.

CHAPTER 8
SALCOMBE TO EXMOUTH

From Salcombe the route is generally north-east all the way to Exmouth. The mouths of the Dart and Teign continue the spectacular series of estuaries. The urban sprawl of Torbay is mitigated by the surprisingly rural and unspoilt countryside on each side of it.

Apart from the castle, already mentioned, there is little visible that is ancient in Salcombe. The reason for this is simple, it is a comparatively modern town. By 1822 it was a fishing town with boatyards. After the trains arrived at Kingsbridge in 1893 it began to develop into a holiday resort and yachting centre. There was in fact a plan to extend the railway here and you can still see where the station was going to be on Snapes Point. The high point of shipbuilding was in the production of fast schooners for the fruit import trade before the days of steam. Because of the perishable nature of their cargo they had to be particularly fast. Salcombe War Memorial pays tribute not only to those who gave their lives in both World Wars, but in addition to the thirteen brave men who lost their lives in a lifeboat disaster in 1916. Leisure sailing is by far the most important plank of the town's prosperity. Unfortunately though,

Looking down the Kingsbridge Estuary towards the sea. The estuary is unusual in that it has no real river flowing into it. Snapes Point middle right was to be the site of Salcombe railway station, but it was never built.

because it is such an attractive place, a surfeit of second homes have had an adverse effect on the town's economy.

Portlemouth is across the estuary from Salcombe and can be reached by passenger ferry. During the Civil War Parliamentary forces erected a battery on Rickham Common to harass the Royalist forces in the castle opposite. Prawle Point is the most southerly point in Devon, in old English it was *Prawhyll* meaning 'lookout', the same use for a thousand years. There was a Lloyd's Signal Station, now a Coast Watch Institution, here and some ships called 'for orders' just as they did at the Lizard. There is a particularly good example of a raised beach, showing how the shoreline has sunk just a little to the west of the Point. The trawler *Yvette* ran ashore here and was never re-floated. A deck hand was in charge, the skipper asleep. The deckhand was worried they were getting inshore but was reluctant to wake the skipper who had a short fuse, until he had made him a cup of tea. While the kettle boiled the inevitable happened and the ship was wrecked. The deckhand was later fined £40 for hazarding his ship! Was that justice?

The path passes above Mattiscombe (pronounced Matchcombe) Beach to round Peartree Point that gives fine views forward to Start Point. Start comes from the Old English for 'tail' as in the bird redstart. The lighthouse here was built in

Mill Bay at East Portlemouth opposite Salcombe. A regular passenger ferry service is not far away.

Start Point in Old English means 'tail' as used in the bird's name Redstart. The Lighthouse was originally built in 1836.

109

The indefatigable Ella Trout whose remarkable life story is told in the book Sisters Against the Sea.

Hallsands pictured before the storm of 1917.

1836 and at first the families lived there even though the children had to go about six miles to school. The path descends towards Hallsands passing through a cherry wood. Arguably this is the only one on the entire Coast Path. How did it get here? By accident, perhaps a bird, or planted with intent; if so for fruit, pipes or furniture? We can only guess. The story of Hallsands is too well known to repeat at length. However, for those who do not know, dredging out at sea lowered the protective beach and during a gale in 1917 the whole village, cottages, store and the London Inn had to be abandoned in the night. The Trout sisters lost their home in the old village but built a hotel above the old village. One of them, Ella, received the OBE for her part in a rescue at sea from the *SS Newholm* which had struck a mine in World War One. Beesands looks inoffensive enough but it was bombed in 1943 and several people were killed. In recent years there have been fears that Beesands might be overwhelmed by the sea, as happened at Hallsands. A massive rock wall was built to prevent this happening. The stone for this coming, perhaps surprisingly, from the Cherbourg peninsula in France! Beesands Ley, which the Ordnance Survey calls Widdicombe Ley, is thought not to be natural, as at Slapton, but created artificially for duck shooting. The houses beyond the ley are called Beesands Cellars, a reminder of past fishing activity, although fishing is continued on a smaller scale at Beesands today.

Torcross was a similar fishing village to Hallsands and Beesands but having had better road communications has grown larger. During World War II this became part of a battle-training area for

D-Day, all the population and their animals being evacuated. The whole idea was a splendid success and no doubt saved countless lives. It is however remembered for one terrible disaster when German E-boats attacked a practice convoy and over 700 US servicemen were killed in one night. A salvaged American Sherman tank stands by the car park as a memorial, and an obelisk of thanks to the inhabitants who were away from their homes for about a year, was erected further along the beach. Slapton Ley is the largest natural freshwater lake in Devon and now forms part of a nature reserve.

The village of Torcross was evacuated for D-Day rehearsals. A Sherman tank by the car park is a reminder of the price paid in human life. Behind the beach on the right is Slapton Ley, the largest natural lake in Devon.

Strete used to be Street but the spelling was changed in 1870 to avoid confusion with Street in Somerset. A Breton force that had landed at Slapton, with the intention of attacking Dartmouth, was engaged at Blackpool Sands in 1404. They were heavily defeated and a te deum in celebration was sung in Westminster Abbey on the orders of Henry IV. Stoke Fleming church was probably built where it is as a daymark for shipping, similar to Wembury. Elias Newcomen is buried here; he was the great grandfather of Thomas Newcomen 1663 –1729 the Dartmouth blacksmith who invented the steam engine. James Watt who often gets credit for inventing steam engines was not born until after Newcomen died.

Slapton memorial

Dartmouth is as interesting as it is scenic. Until the rise of Plymouth it was the most important local port. It was used as an assembly point for the fleets setting out for the Second

111

*Blackpool Sands –
yes the name is
right but a little
different from its
Lancashire name-
sake! A battle was
fought here in 1404
when a Breton force
intent on attacking
Dartmouth was
defeated.*

*Dartmouth's
famous Butterwalk
seen here c.1900.*

and Third Crusades and sent ships to the Siege of Calais. Wine from Bordeaux was important in its early commercial trade, and later it was a major player in the Newfoundland trade. Its most famous merchant was John Hawley who was almost surely the inspiration for the Shipman of Dartmouth in Chaucer's *Canterbury Tales.* Dartmouth has two castles, the older one at the mouth of the river and the later Henry VIII artillery castle at Bayard's Cove. There was heavy fighting here in the Civil War; the Royalists under Prince Maurice capturing it in 1643 and the Parliamentary forces retaking it under Fairfax and Cromwell in 1646. The Rev. John Russell, who gave his name to the breed of terriers, was born here, and the 'Calculating Boy' George Parker Bidder came here to live. In more recent times Dartmouth has been well known for its College, training officers for the Royal Navy, HMS *Britannia.*

Kingswear is across the water from Dartmouth and as close as the trains came. Dartmouth had a station but claimed justly they had never had a train. In or out, you had to use a ferry. Kingswear once had a considerable coal bunkering trade and went on sending coal to the Torquay Gasworks up until 1963. Kingswear was a base for the Free

French Navy in World War II. Now it has a thriving marina. On Froward Point a World War II coastal defence battery has been preserved; it is an interesting comment on technical accomplishment of the time that searchlights had to be positioned in front of the guns. Around Pudcombe Cove there are fruit trees near the path, that were planted to encourage wild birds on the orders of the D'Oyly Carte family who lived at nearby Coleton Fishacre, now owned by the National Trust. Berry Head, shortly before Brixham, was heavily fortified in Napoleonic times; in fact the defences were never used but the garrison would have had the satisfaction of seeing the *Bellerophon* bringing Napoleon Bonaparte into Tor Bay after his final capture, on his way to exile in St Helena. Berry Head House Hotel was originally built as a military hospital and Oxen Cove was where cattle were brought for the fleet when it was victualled in Tor Bay. Berry Head also has a lighthouse that was built as recently as 1906; it claims to be the highest above sea level and the shortest of any lighthouse in England! Brixham was a considerable fishing port in the days of red-sailed trawlers and the business is still continued today by more modern boats.

Until the Dissolution, Paignton was a manor belonging to the Bishop of Exeter. It remained a small place (well known only for its cabbages that were reputed to be very sweet), until the railway came in 1859, thereafter it grew rapidly into

A view of Dartmouth. The big building to the right is HMS Britannia the Royal Navy's officer training school. Before the rise of Plymouth, Dartmouth was the premier port in the area.

Berry Head lighthouse.

113

Roundham Head at
Paignton, with
Goodrington on the
left and Paignton's
harbour on the
right.

Torquay's outer and
inner harbours.

a resort. The arrival of the railway was celebrated by the
making of a gigantic pudding, and this feat has been
repeated once or twice since. The Singer family, the sewing
machine manufacturers, came to live here and built Oldway
Mansion, originally called the 'Wigwam' by locals. A local
entrepreneur Arthur Hyde Denby thought Paignton was
missing out because originally it had no pier. He therefore
bought Teignmouth's but had not thought of the transporta-

tion problems! The present pier was built in 1875. To secure copyright the 'Pirates of Penzance' by Gilbert and Sullivan was first shown at short notice at a little theatre, the Royal Bijou, in Paignton.

Approaching Torquay from Paignton the small headland of Corbyn Head is passed. Sadly a memorial here records the loss of life when a shell misfired during Home Guard practice during World War II. Very soon afterwards, inland across the meadows, can be seen the tithe barn of Torre Abbey. Some have wondered why it was built in front of the Abbey but the reason, no doubt, was to obtain the maximum breeze to assist winnowing in the old fashioned threshing process. The big house next to the barn is the modern Torre Abbey dating from soon after 1598. The remains of the original Torre Abbey, behind, is rather earlier, founded in 1196, it became the richest Premonstratensian (so-called because they originated at Prémontré in France), monastic house in England. Possibly then, English aversion to foreign sounding words may have made many opt for the simpler sounding 'White Canons'! However, if you are looking for something really old in comparatively modern Torquay, visit Kent's Cavern, a local cave and perhaps the earliest know human habitation in Britain. Here remains have been found which may be 450 000 years old; think on this! In Victorian days and a bit later swimming was strictly segregated; the men were banished to far away Meadfoot Beach but the ladies had Beacon Cove nearer the town. Maybe the men had the last laugh as the town fathers allowed the first coal-fired power station to be

Torquay rose to popularity as a tourist resort with the coming of the railway in the 1850s after which the whole of the South Devon coast became a holiday destination. Tourists were keen to visit outlying areas such as Dartmoor with coaches such as this, photographed in 1906, providing daily excursions.

Meadfoot Beach at Torquay. There was once a small harbour here and vestiges can still be seen at low tide. The large white building is Hesketh Crescent built in the 1840s.

In 1885 John 'Babbacombe' Lee was convicted of murdering his employer, Emma Keyse. Sentenced to be hanged the gallows trapdoor three times failed to work and Lee escaped execution. Something of a celebrity, Lee later published his 'true' story.

built on Beacon Quay close to the ladies' beach. The smuts must have been a problem. Torquay is also known as the birthplace of Agatha Christie and the setting for *Fawlty Towers*! Torquay used to be described as an attractive town, perhaps with a Mediterranean look, but in latter years the townscape has been ruined with obtrusive and ugly blocks of flats.

Babbacombe has much else to recommend it but is often remembered most for the murder in 1884 that led to the conviction of John Lee, who was afterwards known as The Man They Could Not Hang. Oddicombe has its cliff railway, opened in 1926, and was possibly the last place to have bathing machines in Torquay. Watcombe was the scene for outdoor concerts in the Valley of Rocks in Victorian days and boasted a film studio after World War II. There is a tunnel at Shaldon that has been reopened, and inevitably it is called 'Smugglers'. Well this could be so but the fact that there is a lime-kiln at the landward entrance to the tunnel makes one think it could have been used for more mundane workaday purposes.

The ferry from Shaldon to Teignmouth claims to be one of, if not the oldest ferry, still to be in operation at a little over a thousand years. Teignmouth is still a port, that was once greatly involved in the Newfoundland trade and was the second oldest holiday resort in Devon, only Exmouth goes back further. It had its own Assembly and Reading Rooms. There used to be horse racing on the Den, the grassy stretch of land between the buildings and the sea. Fanny Burney wrote about donkey and even pig races! Sir Edward Pellew, the naval commander who bombarded Algiers, so freeing Christian slaves, came to live at Bitton House, now municipal offices.

He was made a Viscount and would have liked to have Teignmouth in his title, but it was already in use so he had to settle for being Viscount Exmouth. Edmund Kean the actor played at the theatre here, and John Keats the poet came to stay in 1818 with his invalid brother. Truth to tell he did not like the place its inhabitants or even the weather! The Roman Catholic Church was designed in 1878 by one of the exclusive class of persons whose names appear in English dictionaries. He was Joseph Hansom, the inventor of the Hansom Cab. In World War I Teignmouth was among the places that provided homes for Belgian refugees.

Shaldon ferry is said to have been in operation for over a thousand years, but this 1950s cartoon pokes gentle fun at its character.

The Coast Path leaves Teignmouth along the sea wall. This route has been used by many railway artists and photographers, not to mention countless strollers. Few appreciate why it is there? It was at the Admiralty's insistence that there had to be access to the foreshore in front of the railway. Teignmouth did not realize what an asset it had and for some time never bothered to link the sea wall with their own promenade! Dawlish lies close to Teignmouth and in one respect is similar in that it is a long established resort dating

Looking up the River Teign towards Newton Abbot. Teignmouth is on the right, Shaldon now a suburb on the left. They were proud of the first Shaldon Bridge built across the river, the longest in England, but it only lasted eleven years!

117

*Dawlish seafront.
Above the landward
end of the breakwa-
ter can be seen the
stretch of water
where black swans,
Dawlish's emblem,
live.*

*A steam train
battles through a
storm at Dawlish in
1960.*

from the 1790s. By 1817 it had seven bathing machines 'with proper conductors in attendance, from six o'clock in the morning, till two in the afternoon'. The machines cost 6d to hire June to September but double that October to May! Originally the settlement at Dawlish was about a mile inland, probably for reasons of safety, but as the holiday trade increased, building moved seaward, but happily in a planned fashion, leaving a park with its stream in the centre. It has association with both Jane Austen and Charles Dickens, who chose it as the birthplace for Nicholas Nickleby. In more modern times it has taken up the black swan as its emblem. The black swans originated in Western Australia

but had been introduced to New Zealand in the 1860s and the original Dawlish stock was brought here by a Dawlish man who had emigrated to New Zealand.

Dawlish Warren station was a belated afterthought. The railway opened in 1846 but the station only opened in 1905. The Warren's sandy spit used to have a thriving bungalow settlement with a ferry across to Exmouth. Modern surveys have shown the whole spit is on the move and creeping upriver. Studies are being undertaken to assess this and its implications. Starcross is well known for its atmospheric railway pumping engine house, there is another at Torquay but that one was never used. Much has been written about Brunel's atmospheric railway, some deprecating, calling it a caper. The system undoubtedly failed but against that trains from Exeter to Newton Abbot ran for the best part of a year and the system certainly had advantages. In summer you can still catch the ferry at Starcross across to Exmouth. In winter there is a long diversion up the Exe to Topsham.

Summer holiday-makers at Dawlish Warren, a sandy spit that almost-closes the mouth of the River Exe.

More recently the train line here was washed away in the winter storms of 2014, causing great local resentment for the time it took to restore this vital route to and from the West-country.

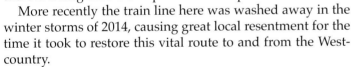

SUGGESTIONS FOR SHORT WALKS

Little Dartmouth

Start at the National Trust Car Park Little Dartmouth 874 492. Walk along bridleway eastwards, only signposted unhelpfully 'Public Bridleway' through the former Little Dartmouth farm to arrive on tarmac behind the old Coastguard Row. Go down the hill to turn right on Coast Path. There is then a long descent; take care at end to keep to the left-hand path. There is a short cut going right but views are poorer. The path comes out just above the sea and you can proceed along to cross a bridge over the sea. You climb steps, and turn right over a stile (if you go ahead for a few yards from the stile you can look down into Compass Cove). Having turned right there is a steep slope and about half way up this the path goes off left. Paths come in from right – ignore. Presently the path goes sharply left, down past a pond and out towards Combe Point, there are several variations but all will get you there. Just before Combe Point there is a large gate, here path goes right. (However, many opt to go left out on to Combe Point for the splendid view.) Continuing westwards along a grassy route; the path turns right. Halfway up the slope a narrow path goes left through gorse, this is narrower but gives better views. If you miss it, it does not matter; at the top you have to turn left and come out at the same point below a gate. The path then simply goes inland along three field edges until you reach the car park. Distance 3½ miles (5.6 km).

Teignmouth – Holcombe Return

Park on Teignmouth seafront, some areas free in winter. Walk to the north-east end where there is a turning circle. Here look at the sea. If the tide is very high, or there is a gale, postpone the walk. From turning circle go slightly left up Eastcliffe Walk. Ignore minor turning forking left to cross railway bridge. At the end of the bridge go left into a park and follow the main gravel path uphill bearing mostly right. Ignore minor path going left to arrive in top corner of park where path goes sharply left, here turn right to go through gap, turn left to proceed up stony track. Ignore footpath signed left; ignore another path signed right to go thorough a kissing gate still proceeding upwards. The path eventually reaches tarmac where you need to turn left. (However, there is a big gate on right which gives views back to the Ness at Shaldon and along the coast to Hope's Nose at Torquay.) After a short distance on tarmac roadway you reach main road practically opposite an old tollhouse. Turn right on Teignmouth Road and cross when able. A little way down the hill, just before a curious thatched building called 'Minadab' turn left and take right fork at Holocene Road. The lane rises and when you are over the crest there are views forward across the mouth of the River Exe to Exmouth. At the bottom of the hill turn right, Hall Lane, ignore left turn called The Orchard to come out on main road. Here cross with care to go down Smugglers Lane. At the bottom go under the railway to climb steps and come out on sea wall. Follow this all the way to Teignmouth. About 3½ miles (5.6 km), but it does depend on where you have parked!

Holcombe Head, once part of the Coast Path, but now walkers are denied its peacefulness and instead have to twice cross a busy main road.

CHAPTER 9
EXMOUTH TO WYKE REGIS

A La Ronde

The whole of this section is aligned along the shores of Lyme Bay. The seaside resorts of Sidmouth and Seaton in East Devon are matched by Lyme Regis in Dorset. The latter part of the route is separated from the true shoreline by the inlets of the West and East Fleets behind the Chesil Bank.

Exmouth was originally, as Leland described, it 'a fisher townlet'. However, from early in the eighteenth century it developed into Devon's first resort, owing much to the proximity of Exeter, then a thriving mercantile and industrial city. Later still it became a small commercial port but the dockyard area has now changed into a marina and housing complex. Local landowners, the Rolle family, put a lot of effort into developing the town. It became a fashionable place to reside and both Lady Nelson and Lady Byron lived here. Set back well from the sea is the National Trust property A La Ronde, an unusual villa to say the least with shell and feather decorated galleries.

Budleigh Salterton is thought of as a nineteenth century resort but in fact goes back at least to the thirteenth century; it was then the location for salt pans as the name suggests.

Exmouth central seafront. Exmouth is the oldest resort in Devonshire thanks to proximity of Exeter once a busy manufacturing and commercial city.

*Looking west to
Budleigh Salterton
across the River
Otter. Recently in
the field bottom
right a Romano-
British dwelling
was discovered.
One part had
underfloor heating,
not bad for say
1800 years ago!*

John Millais lived for a while at 'The Octagon' and a plaque records this fact. He used the seafront as a setting for his famous picture 'The Boyhood of Raleigh'. Raleigh was born not far away at Hayes Barton near East Budleigh. John Millais became a very wealthy man because he was fortunate to be at his peak just as good colour printing was developed. This meant he did not have to rely on selling his originals but could sell many reproductions. Salterton as the locals like to shorten it, rather than Budleigh, used to be used as a warning to statisticians. It had one of the highest death rates in the country, but that did not mean the place was unhealthy, just that it had a very high proportion of retired people in its population. On the other side of the River Otter, inland of

Ladram Bay with its offshore rock stacks. The rocks here were originally laid down in desert conditions and are over 250 million years old, quite the oldest rocks along this coast.

Otterton Ledge, a few years ago a tile was found and a quick excavation revealed a small Romano-British villa. There were two buildings, one sparsely built, probably used for farming, and the other had a hypocaust, underfloor heating nearly two thousand years ago! If you have just walked the two extra miles round via White Bridge reflect on the fact that some years ago a donor offered to have a footbridge built across the mouth of the River Otter at his expense and give it to Budleigh Salterton. His offer was turned down as the Council did not like the way he had made his money – in trade!

Ladram Bay is well known for its terracotta-coloured rock stacks. Originally laid down in desert conditions they are over 250 million years old, the oldest rocks along this coast.

The Promenade at Budleigh Salterton c.1910.

Sidmouth is a genteel resort and is remembered for a certain Princess Victoria who stayed here before she began her long reign. The photograph shows Sidmouth seafront; note the groyne off shore. Groynes were built to prevent erosion on the beach but some think they have caused other problems.

Elizabeth Barrett Browning.

The wreck of the MSC Napoli that grounded in 2007 and proved obdurate to shift necessitating unloading of cargo at sea.

High Peak was a Neolithic settlement and used to offer superb distance views of Dartmoor, that is until it was afforested making access difficult. Sidmouth was another small fishing and market town until it was developed as a resort. George III reportedly 'discovered Devon' when he paid a visit to Sidmouth in 1791, but for some reason it never attracted the attention which his bathing did at Weymouth. Elizabeth Barrett Browning stayed here for a few years. A more modern literary figure, who lived in Sidmouth, was R. F. Delderfield one of whose best known works was *A Horseman Riding By* which was also made into a television serial. The railway was late coming in 1874 and the towns-folk did their best to nullify its arrival by keeping the station well away from the town. Happily for those who like the status quo, sadly for those who like their towns to grow. For those who like their beaches uncrowded Weston Mouth is the one to try. True it is only pebbles and has no sand, but the car park being about a mile away, and a mere hundred or so steps, does deter the crowds!

The attractive village of Branscombe with its church containing a three-decker pulpit is inland, but the Coast Path goes down to Branscombe Mouth. Today Branscombe is chiefly remembered for the wreck of the MSC *Napoli* in 2007 and the visitations of looters, or should we call them modern wreckers. Beyond Branscombe Mouth is the first sizeable area of landslip that collapsed in 1791.

Looking down into the cove at Beer.

Beer had two traditional occupations, fishing and lace-making. The former is still carried on despite the difficult conditions caused by the lack of a harbour. The making of Honiton lace that was once commonplace has now gone. In the early seventeenth century this area was one of the most important for manufacturing lace in Devon and the tradition continued for centuries. Queen Victoria's wedding dress was made here, an accolade to local standards. Seaton was another town that has moved seaward as the holiday industry grew and the risk of raiders diminished. The Romans came here and built a substantial villa, but it is now known from archaeological work that the site the Romans took over was occupied for a long time before they came. In modern times Seaton has become known for its tramway. It used to be at Eastbourne but it had difficulties with planning so it moved here instead. Seaton's gain was Eastbourne's loss!

Axmouth is ancient and interesting. It was the terminus of a Roman road, but whether this was the end of the Fosse Way is an open question. It was an early Saxon settlement and was a port up until medieval times. It should of course be understood that the River Axe was once considerably wider and open to vessels further upstream than it is now. However, problems arose with a pebble bar blocking the river. Over the centuries various attempts were made to redress this, right up until the railway came. The old road bridge still used for the Coast Path is the oldest extant

concrete bridge in the country, dating from 1877. When it was being built it was designed as though of stone to disguise the concrete. If the builders had realized how successful they would be and how long their work would last one wonders if they would have done this? Many folk cross over and miss the little tollhouse on the western side erected to collect bridge tolls. Are you surprised this was also made of concrete? Shortly after Axmouth follows an even larger area of landslip that occurred in 1839. As it happened the President of the Geological Society was staying in the vicinity at the time so it was very well documented. Just at the end of the landslip, and shortly before Lyme Regis, the border between Devon and Dorset is crossed.

Lyme Regis, the Lyme part of the name comes from the fact that it is on the River Lim, the Regis refers to the granting of a Royal charter by King Edward I. Daniel Defoe wrote in his *Tour* first published 1724: 'This is a town of good fortune and has in it several eminent merchants who carry on a considerable trade to France, Spain, Newfoundland'. He went on to write 'they have neither creek or bay, road, or river, they have a good harbour; but 'tis such a one as is in all Britain besides'.

He was of course referring to the Cobb. Thomas Coram the philanthropist was born in the area and is best known for setting up the Foundling Hospital that opened in London in 1741. We tend to think of packhorses as a slow method of transport, but such transport could be speeded up by changes of horses and travelling day and night. *The Diary of Walter Young* (Camden Society), 1848, gives an interesting example, describing the fish-jobbers coming down to the beach at Lyme Regis with their strings of horses tied tail to tail, the

When walking the Coast Path in the usual anti-clock-wise direction Lyme Regis is the first town in Dorset, being just over the border from Devon.

Donkeys, beach tents and crowds of visitors enjoying the summer of 1914.

Mary Anning

St Catherine's Chapel standing on its hill in front of Abbotsbury. The date of the chapel's building is not recorded but its ornate style may indicate the early fourteenth century. Abbotsbury's name derives from the Benedictine Abbey founded here by King Canute. Little remains of the once great Abbey, except for its massive tithe barn.

loading of the baskets and the departure of the train of horses, at a gallop, for London. The area around Lyme is famous for its fossils and one name above all is associated with them. This is Mary Anning a poor local girl who, aged twelve, found the first complete Ichthyosaurus, a large Jurassic reptile. What is sometimes not realized is that Mary devoted her life to fossils, making several more significant discoveries.

Charmouth is chiefly remembered for the visit of Catherine of Aragon in 1501 when she is reputed to have stayed at an inn here. She came and married Prince Arthur, but he died in the following year so Catherine later became the first wife of Henry VIII. The future Charles II paid a much more furtive visit in disguise in 1651 after his defeat at the Battle of Worcester, when he was attempting to flee the country. He was unsuccessful here, but eventually got away from Brighton. Eype (meaning steep) Mouth has as a relic of World War II several tank traps that were figuratively known as 'Dragon's Teeth'. Spin is often regarded as a modern departure, this is just not so. In the nineteenth century when the railway was imminently expected, in 1884, it was decided that the name Bridport harbour was not going to attract visitors – so the name was changed to West Bay, and that is what it has been called to this day, even though the railway has long closed. Because of the proximity of the important rope-making town of Bridport a number of attempts have been made over the centuries to build and maintain an effective harbour here. These developments have continued right into the twenty-first century.

Abbotsbury, today known best for its swannery, was once much better known for its Abbey from which the place derives its name. It was a Benedictine house founded in the reign of King Canute and continued for some five hundred years until the Dissolution when the black-robed monks were dispersed. There is very little of the Abbey buildings remaining except for the massive tithe barn that was one of the largest in the country. What most walkers will have noticed is St Catherine's Chapel perched high on its hill, presumably as a daymark. Its exact date of building is not known but assumed to be the fourteenth century. Yet it seems unlikely that such an extravagant form of construction would have been built after the Black Death, so maybe it was built just before then, In front of the chapel are a series of strip lynchets, an ancient form of terrace cultivation. The West Fleet was used in World War II as a practise area for the 'bouncing bomb', developed by the inventor Barnes Wallis for the air raid on the Mohne and Eder Dams in 1943. At East Fleet there is half a church! Or more correctly just the chancel is left. The rest was swept away when the sea broke through the Chesil Beach in a great gale in 1824. The Chesil Beach is often called Chesil Bank, which seems a more apt description. It is 18 miles long, 220 yards wide at its widest and over 50 feet tall at its highest point, and the size of pebble diminishes all the way from Portland to its western end. It was claimed that local fishermen landing on it could tell how far they were along it by looking at the size of the pebbles. On a sadder note it has been the scene of many a shipwreck with vessels driven by storm on to the Bank. The exact origin of the Bank is still a matter of debate.

As you come towards the end of Lyme Bay it may be interesting to recall that in 1940 in the projected German 'Operation Sea Lion', the invasion of England, planned that the most western arm of attack would come ashore here, in August or early September, and drive north towards Bristol. However, in mid-September, after the RAF's success in the Battle of Britain, Hitler called the invasion off.

This view looking from east to west along the Chesil Bank shows clearly its nature. The pebbles grow progressively smaller along the length from east to west. Its breadth at its widest is 660 yards (200m) and at its highest, its height reaches 50 feet (15m), an awful lot of pebbles! And a taxing walk!

SUGGESTIONS FOR SHORT WALKS

Otterton circuit

Park near the entrance to South Farm 076 831 on the east bank of the River Otter near Budleigh Salterton. Walk back along the road crossing the bridge over the river to turn immediately right signposted Otterton 1½ miles. Walk upstream alongside river, ignoring paths away from or across river. When you reach the tarmac road at Otterton turn right crossing the bridge into the village. Proceed along main street, then for a while there is a pleasant pavement walk between houses and stream. At junction take right fork signed Ladram Bay, named Bell Street going uphill. Just after a 30mph sign, fork right again and go over cross roads continuing up to Stantyway Farm, a big building on right. Here turn left taking path signed 'To the Coast Path' that is tarmac as far as Monks Wall, a private house, here you leave the tarmac for a footpath. Follow this to the coast where turn right on Coast Path signposted Budleigh Salterton. The Coast Path continues to the mouth of the River Otter where you turn inland following well used path back to your parked car. Distance 6 miles (9.6 km).

The South West Coast Path hugs the cliff edge on the route between Budleigh Salterton and Ladram Bay.

Branscombe Mouth – landslip.

Park at the car park at Branscombe Mouth. Cross the road by the water splash to take the path up the hill signposted Coast Path Beer. Shortly the Coast Path goes right but keep on up the hill to the left signposted Hooken Cliff ½ mile, eventually reaching the top. Here go forward keeping near the cliff top. Presently you pass a watch house and still keep by the cliff to go through a gap of an old hedge and very soon, a kissing gate. Now be sure you keep with cliff edge, a broad path goes slightly left but it is not what you want. Continuing with cliff edge you descend into a dip where you turn back right on to the Coast Path signposted, 'Branscombe Mouth'. You then descend into landslip or undercliff area. Later there are one or two paths going down to beach but keep on through the landslip area. The last few yards become a track through a chalet area but you soon cross a cattle grid to descend again to Branscombe Mouth. Distance, less than 2½ miles (4 km).

CHAPTER 10
WYKE REGIS TO POOLE HARBOUR

The last section of the path girdles the Isle of Portland and then the route goes eastwards to turn north just before Swanage, and then continues north for the last few miles of the path to South Haven Point. Portland provides a spectacular, mostly high level, walk. Ballard Down between Swanage and Studland is the last of the great viewpoints on the path with an enormous vista of Poole Harbour.

Wyke Regis today is just a suburb of Weymouth. It was, however, a separate entity for centuries. Another important change is the main road to Portland. Access to Portland had always been by boat or ferry from Wyke Regis. It was only an act of Parliament in 1835 that led to the building of a bridge across the entrance to the East Fleet so at long last giving access by road. Later a rail bridge was built and train services started in 1865, only to finish a hundred years later.

Portland is known for many things to different people; yet there is one very common misconception because it is called the Isle of Portland it is assumed to be an island. It is not, being joined to the mainland by the Chesil Beach. In ancient times it was the source of Portland chert (a form of quartz) stone tools, These have been found not only in Dorset, but Somerset, Devon and Cornwall, as far indeed as the Land's

The north of the so-called Isle of Portland, though until the bridge enacted by Parliament in 1835 was built, the commonest way to visit Portland was to use the ferry from Wyke Regis. The bottom of the picture shows the Chesil Bank near its southeast extremity, sheltering as it does the village of Chesil. Portland Harbour is to the upper left. The old forts on the high ground further to the right are now used for prison accommodation. At the top of the picture the mainland Dorset coast can be seen stretching away into the distance.

End peninsula. For centuries, right up until the present time it has been the source of Portland Stone for building purposes. Portland Cement, incidentally, invented by Joseph Aspdin in 1824, is only called that because when it sets it looks like Portland Stone.

Portland was the site for another of Henry VIII's artillery castles, and the one at Portland is well preserved. In fact if you want to get some idea as to how they were planned and operated; this is the one to visit. The English Admiral Robert Blake won a considerable victory against the Dutch under Van Tromp off Portland in 1653. Later it was to become an important naval base, closed in 1995, and the huge breakwater, built by convict labour, lets it lay claim to having the largest artificial harbour in Britain. Of relatively modern naval history is a section of Mulberry Harbour just off the north coast. These sections were used to build prefabricated ports off the coast of Normandy after D-Day. Of agricultural interest are the vestiges of strip cultivation and the eponymous breed of sheep. These sheep were once plentiful on Portland but recently have been absent. Luckily the breed has been saved from extinction.

Malefactors have cause to remember the name as it has a long record of prison and borstal establishments, including once a floating prison. It was popular for penal restraint because, of course, escape routes were limited. Portland also gained notoriety when two

The 'harbour fleet' of fishing boats drawn up along Castletown Strip, Portland, in 1891.

clerks at the Underwater Weapons Establishment started selling secrets; they received a sentence of fifteen years apiece. Portland was the last stop on the calendar of the West Country travelling fairground's route. They would end up here each November and usually, because of their windy pitch down Easton main street, would be glad to close.

Chiswell is the first settlement reached on the 'island' and was the original railway terminus. On a winter's evening it was an incongruous sight to see engines, their fireboxes aglow, blow off steam here apparently in the town square. The steep climb up towards Portland Heights should give you plenty of excuse to stop and turn round to admire the expanding view behind you. There are those who regard this as one of the classic viewpoints in England. Shortly before Portland Bill is the well-known Pulpit Rock, a post-quarrying feature. At Portland Bill there were two previous lighthouses but the present one was built in 1905. Note here the old derricks that once loaded ships with stone. Shortly after the Bill, in one of the old lighthouses, is a bird observatory, this being a splendid place for watching bird migration. Just north of Church Ope Cove is Rufus Castle. Despite the name there is no direct evidence to link it with William II but it certainly has a record from 1142 just two reigns later when it was captured from King Stephen. Verne Prison was originally built as a commanding fortress to defend Portland Harbour.

Assuming you have circumnavigated Portland success-fully you will come back via Ferry Bridge to the mainland at Wyke Regis. Sandsfoot Castle, another Henry VIII artillery

Quarrymen at work beneath the ruined Rufus Castle drawn as an archetypal medieval ruin by J.M.W. Turner in 1849.

The Chesil across the top, Portland Harbour to the left and the River Wey forming Weymouth Harbour is the inlet on the right. The prominent building on the little penin-sula alongside Weymouth Harbour is Nothe Fort.

Thomas Hardy

Weymouth from the east. The modern town grew from an amalgamation of Melcombe Regis and Weymouth in 1571. It developed into a resort in the late eighteenth century. Thomas Hardy called it Budmouth in his novels.

castle, was built as a twin to Portland but it is not in a good state of preservation. Some of it, in fact, has fallen into the sea. The path continues to go through the Nothe Gardens a delightful place near the entrance to Weymouth's Harbour. Nothe Fort was built in answer to threats from the French in 1872; there had however been defensive works on such a strategic site previously. It is now regularly open to visitors. In summer you have the option of crossing Weymouth Harbour, the estuary of the River Wey, by passenger ferry.

In Roman times a road linking Ilchester to Dorchester continued on to a port near modern Weymouth at Radipole. Two towns later grew up here, Weymouth itself to the south of the river Wey and Melcombe Regis to the north; both dating from the early Middle Ages, they became one township in 1571. In the late eighteenth century the town made a name for itself as it developed into a resort under Royal patronage. Thomas Hardy often stayed here and wrote about the town in his works, calling it Budmouth. Weymouth in World War II became a major embarkation area for the D-Day invasion.

Very close to Weymouth is the Radipole Lake Nature Reserve with its large reed-bed habitat. Just beyond the southern end of Preston is the Romano-British temple at Jourdans, dating principally from the fourth century. You would expect such a site to be protected, but what may surprise you is that the next big holiday camp at Bowleaze Cove, and 1500 years younger, is also protected, as it has unusual panoramic windows! The White Horse with rider that can be seen in several places from the Coast Path represents George III. It was cut out in 1815 and it has amused some that he is shown departing from Weymouth rather than going to it!

The figure of George III cut into the chalk near Bowleaze Cove.

Ringstead has a deserted village just a little way inland. It was possibly abandoned because of the Black Death, but there are other theories. Later the area was partly forbidden territory because of a large radar site. As you ascend from Ringstead Bay you pass an area called the Burning Cliff. In 1882 spontaneous combustion in iron pyrites set alight oil shales here that burnt for at least a year and smoldered longer. It became a popular tourist sight despite its unpleasant smell. Beyond is the little wooden chapel of St Catherine's at Holworth; behind it is a small graveyard looking out on the sea. From the chapel you ascend White Noethe a grand viewpoint and the former site of a row of coastguard cottages. Durdle Door, the natural rock arch probably means 'pierced' and then 'opening' or a door. At Hanbury Tout excavations of a bell barrow yielded a crouched skeleton burial. Lulworth Cove's horseshoe shaped bay is a well-known and popular spot. Not everyone appreciates that its shape came about because there is a hard band of limestone rock to seaward but a softer infill behind. This meant that once the outer band was pierced erosion was much faster behind it, leading to the cove's horseshoe shape. Lulworth has an unusual claim to fame as it has a butterfly, true only a small one, called after it. This is the Lulworth Skipper, first recognized as a

The Durdle Door natural arch, a well-known feature of this coast. Unfortunately it has recently been in the news because of people seriously injuring themselves by jumping off its top into the sea.

Lulworth Cove where the sea cutting through a hard band of rock has hollowed out a horseshoe shaped bay in the softer material behind.

St Mary's church, East Lulworth

separate species in 1882 at Durdle Door. There have been boat trips from here going well back to the days of paddle steamers, the trips continue today and in recent years diving has become popular. Unfortunately like Salcombe the community suffers from a high proportion of second homes.

From the top of Bindon Hill there are deservedly good views. It is possible to see Bournemouth, beyond the end of the path – encouragement indeed. Much nearer are views of East Lulworth. St Mary's, the Roman Catholic Church, was the first church of that persuasion to be built after the Reformation. George III gave permission to Thomas Weld apparently on the condition that the church looked like a house, not a church. The Castle was burnt down in 1929 and has since been rebuilt.

Worbarrow Tout provides a pleasant diversion for those who have the strength. Someone once called it a miniature Gibraltar and obviously in the past the viewpoint was well used because there are residual brick steps up it. Around here has been found evidence of former salt extraction by boiling seawater.

Tyneham a little inland is again a diversion but many take it. It is an old settlement mentioned in Domesday but was compulsorily evacuated at short notice in World War II. Reasonable in view of the emergency then, but not so reasonably the village was not returned to the owners after the war.

Kimmeridge is an area with oil-bearing shales. Historically they were used as a cheap form of fuel both for salt-boiling and in poor households in the Swanage area. In modern times Kimmeridge became the richest on-shore oil well in England, until superceded by Wytch Farm near Poole Harbour. Kimmeridge was also known for its slate, some of which was used on the local church. More intriguing a series of round discs have been found and called 'Kimmeridge money'. It does not seem likely that it really was currency but more possibly the end pieces of slate worked on lathes. One of the items made on the lathes were bracelets, some of which have been found at Hadrian's Wall!

The Clavell Tower was moved inland in 2007–8 to safeguard it from falling into the sea. It appears in the work of Thomas Hardy but also more recently in *The Black Tower* by P. D. James. The one advantage of the new poorer path up on to St Aldhelm's or St Alban's Head is that you pass the Royal Marines memorial with its little garden. It has been erected to remember those Royal Marines killed since World War II. The inscription finishes with the lines 'Rest awhile and reflect that we who are living can enjoy the beauty of the sea and countryside'.

St Aldhelm's chapel

In the foreground St Aldhelm's or St Alban's head, the sweep of Swanage Bay behind and, beyond, Ballard Down, Studland Bay, and then Bournemouth. The complex of buildings bottom left was the old coastguard station to its right the square building is the old chapel.

137

The radar memorial on St Alban's Head.

On top of the Head there are three items of interest, a chapel, the one time coastguard row and a modern radar memorial. Pevsner speculates whether or not it was originally built as a chapel. One thing is certain, that it has been a chapel for a very long time because we know a chaplain was appointed in the thirteenth century. The dedication to St Aldhelm is to the first Saxon bishop of Sherborne (c.640–709). The chapel used to be a bit neglected but in recent years it has been kept very well, usually even having fresh flowers for decoration. The coastguard row was built in 1834 and has of course now changed use. The memorial commemorates the pioneer work on radar 1941–42. The next stretch of the coast was once the scene of many coastal quarries. Winspit was the last one to close but there are doubts as to the date. One source says 1945 another claims it went on into the 1950s. What we do know is that there were many quarries and they worked for many centuries in the past. Defoe for instance wrote of 'vast quarreys of stone, which is cut flat, and us'd in London in great quantities for paving courtyards, alleys, avenues to houses, kitchens, footways on the sides of the high-streets and the like'.

Poole is top right, at middle centre is Brownsea Island, a refuge for our native Red Squirrel. At the bottom right is the Sandbanks peninsula notorious for its extravagantly high property prices.

Anvil Point has a lighthouse opened in 1881. Close by are another pair of nautical mile markers, similar in function to those on Whitsand Bay in Cornwall. At Durlston Head is a stone globe on it correct axis, it would hardly be as portable as a map at some 40 odd tons! Close by is Durlston Castle,

originally built as a restaurant about 1890. The Victorian George Burt built both the Globe and Castle. He was a local Swanage man of humble beginnings, who by hard work achieved much; he built up a considerable paving business in London and later became a property developer.

Swanage, or at least Swanage Bay, made news early when a fleet of King Alfred's defeated the Danes in 877. Swanage has a mention in Domesday and was for a long time a small fishing port. It became busy shipping stone from the local quarries principally to London. This considerable coastwise trade continued up until the railway arrived about 1880. After the visit of Princess Victoria in 1833 the town progressively changed to a holiday resort which it is today.

The last serious climb of the path takes you up on to Ballard Down. There will be few walkers who do not wish to pause here to look at the panorama of Poole Harbour, not to mention the end of the path at South Haven Point! Then it is down past Old Harry Rocks to Studland that has a remarkable largely Norman Church. From nearly the other end of the time-scale it has a World War II fortification, called Fort Henry, built by Canadian engineers. The end is near now but unless you divert through the nature reserve you will have to brave the naturist's beach. That hazard overcome, it is on to the End Marker and even if you omit the photo opportunity it is still a wonderful feeling to have completed the South West Coast Path!

South West Coast Path marker

SUGGESTIONS FOR SHORT WALKS

Portland West Coast
Park at car park at Portland Heights 691 731, walk back to main road and round the corner to catch a bus to Portland Bill. Be warned services to the Bill are less frequent than those to Southwell so it is worth planning to catch the bus you want.

Get off at the Bill; walk down past the lighthouse with its red ring, to the Trinity House 1844 obelisk. Here turn right, shortly nearly opposite the Pulpit Rock you have to turn right to avoid wire fenced defence establishment. Presently the path comes back to the coast and then you walk along the

Portland Bill lighthouse

Potential thrills on Studland Beach!

length of the west coast the scenery improving as you go. You pass a large sign for 'Tout Quarry' and then come to a much smaller sign 'New Ground Easton' here turn right on tarmac to come to a crane beside the main road. Cross with care and go up the hill to the roundabout and then back to the car park at Portland Heights. Distance about 4 miles (6.4 km).

Ballard Down – Studland
Park in car park at Studland nearest Redend Point 036 828, it is a National Trust car park and they call it Middle Beach. Walk back to main road by coming out of the car park and in a few yards forking right, this is Beach Road but it does not tell you that until you reach the top. At the top opposite public toilets fork right again for a few yards to bus stop. Catch Swanage bus alighting at 'Ulwell Lane/Currendon Hill' that is the stop before Ulwell. Go over the stile close to the bus stop, sign-posted Purbeck Way Coast Path 1¾ and having gone a few yards you are sign-posted right through a wood. Soon after a kissing gate there is a footpath going left look for low marker directing you to the Obelisk. Then there is steep climb over 200 steps and a further climb to the obelisk. Here turn right and walk along the top to Ballard Down to the sea. (Here you have a most superb panoramic view of Poole Harbour). On reaching Coast Path turn left descending to above Old Harry Rocks. (The mainland equivalent of The Needles on the Isle of Wight). Turn west here, you have to, and follow Coast Path back to Studland. Watch for sign slightly off path 'Alternative Coast Path South Beach', take this. The path goes down to the beach walk along past beach huts and the bottom of a sandy lane where there is a café, Then go forward on beach but watch for another low marker on left between beach huts. Look carefully for this, it is easy to miss. Then walk up path shortly passing the wartime blockhouse Fort Henry to return to the car park. About 4½ miles (7.2 km).

BIBLIOGRAPHY

Books
Ayto, John and Crofton, Ian, *Brewer's Britain & Ireland* (2005)
Cherry, Bridget and Pevsner, Nikolaus, *The Buildings of England Devon* (1997)
Carter, Philip *The South west Coast Path - An Illustrated History* (2005)
Collings, A G *Along the South West Way* Part 1 Minehead to Bude (1986)
Cornish Federation of Women's Institutes *The Cornwall Village Book* (1991)
Devon Federation of Women's Institutes *The Devon Village Book* (1990)
Hoskins W G *Devon* (1954)
Jennett, Sean ed. *Cornwall and the Isles of Scilly* (1965)
Newman, John, and Pevsner, Nikolaus, *The Buildings of England Dorset* (1999)
Pevsner, Nilolaus, *The Buildings of England Cornwall* (1996)
Richards, Mark, *Walking the North Cornwall Coastal Footpath* (1974)
South West Coast Path Association *A History* (1998)

National Trail Guides
They are presently all called *South West Coast Path* and the four titles are: Minehead to Padstow, Padstow to Falmouth, Falmouth to Exmouth and Exmouth to Poole.

South West Coast Path Association
Annual Guide, The Complete Guide to the Longest National Trail. A reverse guide is re-issued periodically. The Association also produces over 50 *Path Descriptions* that cover the whole path and are up-to-date detailed descriptions of short lengths of the path.

INDEX